D1639407

EAST SUSSEX COUNTY COUNCIL
WITHDRAWN
2 1 JUN 2024
20

04473376

SUSHI
taste and technique

SUSHI

taste and technique

KIMIKO BARBER and HIROKI TAKEMURA

CONTENTS

WHAT IS SUSHI?

a history of sushi

The simple definition of sushi is "vinegared rice with a filling or topping of raw, cooked, cured, or marinated fish, shellfish, vegetables, or egg". It is eaten as a snack, a starter, or as a main course and comes in many different forms, from bowls of rice scattered with fish and vegetables to rolled, pressed, and hand-formed sushi. In Japan, sushi is extremely popular; it is enjoyed not only in sushi bars but also at home by the whole family. Globally, it is Japan's most famous food – indeed, a Japanese ambassador once joked that sushi had done more to raise the international profile of Japan than the country's official efforts.

▲ **RICE FARMING**
Rice is still a staple food of Japan, thousands of years after its introduction in around 500BCE.

THE ORIGINS OF SUSHI

No one knows exactly when sushi was invented, but it is thought to have originated as a way of preserving food in the rice-growing regions of Southeast Asia. Meat, fish, or vegetables were salted and packed into wooden presses with cooked rice and left to ferment naturally – the carbohydrate in the rice would convert to lactic acid and, together with the salt, would pickle the food. Some academics believe that sushi came to Japan with the introduction of rice cultivation from China, as early as 500BCE, while others think that the practice was brought back by Buddhist priests returning from China after their training in the 7th century CE.

The first records of this early form of sushi – fish preserved in fermented rice – were found at the ancient land-bound capital, Heijō-kyō (modern-day Nara), where it was sent as a form of tax payment from the coastal regions. Today, examples of fermented sushi, known as *nare zushi*,

The shorter fermentation period still preserved the fish, but the fermented rice would remain instead of breaking down entirely. This new type of sushi was called *nama-nare zushi*, meaning fresh-fermented sushi, or *han-nare zushi*, half-fermented sushi. By this time, sushi was being made widely by ordinary people, to whom rice was a food not to be wasted. The acidic-tasting rice was now eaten with the fish, a familiar idea that still applies to the sushi we know and eat today.

SUSHI EVOLVES

Japan saw a major change in political power at the start of the 17th century, which was to have a far-reaching influence on its cuisine. In 1603, shogun Tokugawa Ieyasu unified the country and established a federal government in Edo (now Tokyo). With the establishment of a powerful political and social structure came economic growth, fuelled by a focus on boosting rice agriculture – it is estimated that rice production almost doubled.

The increased rice production led to the wider use of other rice-based products, too, such as sake and rice vinegar. It was the greater availability of rice vinegar specifically that resulted in the birth of *haya zushi*, or "fast sushi". Instead of letting rice ferment naturally and produce lactic acid, rice vinegar was now added to it, which reduced the time it took to prepare sushi from several months to just a few hours.

Using vinegar to season the rice not only made sushi quicker to make, it also encouraged the creation of new styles of sushi. It was no longer essential to press the rice and fish into a box to ferment it (although pressed sushi continued to be very popular). Over the next couple of

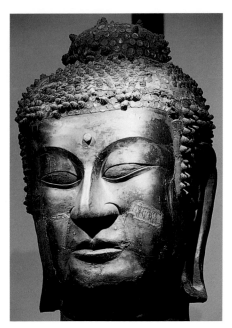

▲ **THE SPREAD OF KNOWLEDGE**
Buddhist priests may have brought sushi back from China in the 7th century CE.

can still be found all over Japan. The most famous example is *funa zushi*, which is made from carp found in Lake Biwa near Kyoto. The fish and rice are pressed into layers and fermented for at least a year (sometimes two years or more). By the time it is ready to eat, there is almost no rice left, only extremely pungent-smelling fish. Something of an acquired taste, it is best described as a mixture of very mature Camembert cheese and Thai fish sauce.

FROM PRESERVED FISH TO SUSHI

Nare zushi continued in its original form until the mid-15th century, when the process was revolutionized by reducing the fermentation period to less than six months.

CONTINUED ▶

centuries, many other types of sushi evolved, such as *chirashi zushi* (scattered sushi), *maki zushi* (rolled sushi), and *inari zushi* (sushi stuffed into seasoned, deep-fried tofu pouches). By the end of the 18th century, these new styles of sushi were being made in all corners of Japan.

NIGIRI ZUSHI – THE FIRST FAST FOOD

Hanaya Yohei, who set up a sushi stall in Edo in the early 19th century, is widely credited with being the inventor of the *nigiri zushi*, or hand-formed sushi, that we know today. He was the first chef to squeeze vinegared rice into a ball and top it with a slice of fish. Although the addition of rice vinegar had reduced preparation time, sushi chefs still made

traditional pressed sushi, which took some time to prepare. The residents of Edo were notoriously impatient, so Yohei's newly invented *nigiri zushi*, which took only a few minutes to prepare, soon caught on. The new style of sushi was known as *Edomae nigiri*, or "Tokyo-style hand-formed sushi", and local fish and shellfish from Tokyo Bay were used for its toppings. It was much larger in size than modern *nigiri zushi*, however, and the toppings were mostly cooked, cured, or marinated – not raw as we are familiar with today.

As popular as it was in Edo (later renamed Tokyo), *nigiri zushi* was only made in the Tokyo area until the 1940s. At the end of World War II, food rationing prevented sushi shops from operating normally. When the Allied Occupation authorities issued a directive allowing the exchange of one cup of rice for 10 pieces of *nigiri zushi* and a sushi roll, they did not include any other type of sushi. To keep their shops open, sushi chefs in the rest of Japan found it necessary to adopt Tokyo-style hand-formed sushi.

SUSHI STALLS DISAPPEAR

It was at about this time that sushi stalls began to disappear completely. Sushi stalls had been familiar features on Tokyo street corners throughout the previous centuries, when they were hauled into their alloted place in the evenings, stategically positioned to catch hungry men on their way back from public bath houses. Customers shared communal bowls of pickled ginger and soy sauce and wiped their hands on a curtain

◄ **URBAN FAST FOOD**
The quick pace of life in Edo (now Tokyo) gave rise to the first fast food – *nigiri zushi*.

▲ ANCIENT ORIGINS
Pressed sushi is the oldest form of sushi but almost disappeared after World War II.

▲ MODERN INTERPRETATIONS
Sushi burrito is one of the new styles of sushi emerging with sushi's global popularity.

hung behind them. A sure sign of a good sushi stall was a filthy curtain, as this showed that a lot of hungry diners had eaten there. With the demise of public bath houses and tightening of food hygiene regulations, the stalls gave way to sushi shops that were open during the day. By the late 1950s, the invention of *kaiten zushi*, or conveyor-belt sushi, had arrived, making sushi more affordable and accessible than ever.

SUSHI TODAY

Sushi has come a long way since its origins as a means of preserving fish, and continues to evolve and develop further. Sushi chefs – both Japanese and non-Japanese, especially those in the USA – are creating innovative new styles of sushi that incorporate Western techniques and ingredients, such as sushi burritos and sandwiches. Sushi has also led the way in gaining worldwide popularity and recognition for Japanese food, and in 2013, *washoku*, Japanese cuisine, was awarded UNESCO world heritage status.

With this new recognition, Japanese ingredients are becoming more available, and there is no better time for making sushi at home. Although it is easy to buy ready-prepared sushi, nothing compares to enjoying fresh, homemade sushi with your family and friends.

SUSHI ETIQUETTE
dos and don'ts

There is something about the formal and orderly appearance of sushi that can make some people feel awkward. Luckily, there are no strict rules of conduct, but feeling at ease with the etiquette will not only help you relax, it will enhance your enjoyment of the meal. Sushi bars in Japan are intimate but relaxed places; proceed in the same vein when enjoying sushi at home.

STRUCTURING THE MEAL

At sushi bars, the absence of a menu means that there is no obvious meal structure. Similarly, when making sushi at home, there are no rules about what selection to offer and no set order in which to eat sushi.

Choose whatever takes your fancy and consider these conventional guidelines, but don't regard them as gospel:

• The Japanese often serve soup at both ends of the meal. Traditionally, *sui mono*, which is similar to consommé, is served at the start. *Miso shiru*, or miso soup, usually signifies the end of a meal (see pp.52–55 for soups).

• A few slices of sashimi can be a gentle start to a sushi meal.

• Begin with omelette, as its subtle flavour allows you to taste the rice. However, I have known sushi gurus to end a meal with omelette, treating it like a sweet dessert.

• A logical (but not essential) approach is to start with blander-tasting white fish and work your way towards richer fish with red meat and more strongly flavoured toppings. However, if your favourite topping is fatty belly of tuna, it is fine to start with that.

• Some say that you should finish a meal with rolled sushi. This may be because they contain more rice and are therefore more filling than hand-formed sushi, but I don't think you should have to wait.

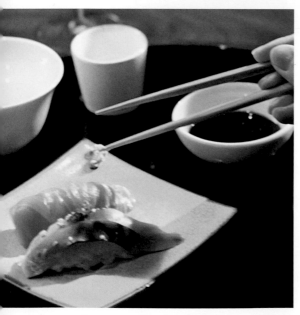

STRONGLY FLAVOURED TOPPINGS

CHOPSTICK ETIQUETTE

Provide chopsticks, a chopstick holder, and a small dipping bowl at each place setting. If you are using disposable wooden chopsticks in a paper sleeve, take the chopsticks out of the sleeve, break them apart, and place them on the small chopstick rest in front of you as you take your seat.

• Use a small individual bowl for dipping your own sushi.

• Don't pass food from your chopsticks to another person's chopsticks as this is considered to be extremely bad luck. (In the traditional Japanese funeral ceremony, relatives pass the cremated bones of the deceased with chopsticks before collecting them in a burial pot.)

• If you are helping yourself to food from a communal plate or serving someone else, it is polite to turn your chopsticks around and use the top ends.

DIPPING SUSHI IN AN INDIVIDUAL BOWL

CHOPSTICKS OR FINGERS?

If you don't feel comfortable using chopsticks, it is perfectly acceptable to use your fingers (see p.12, how to dip hand-formed sushi). Hand-formed sushi, or *nigiri zushi*, was originally invented as a snack to be eaten at a street stall. At a sushi bar, you are given a wet towel at the start of a meal to wipe your fingers on before you begin; you can do the same at home.

EATING SUSHI WITH FINGERS

CONTINUED ▶

THE CORRECT USE OF SOY SAUCE

One of the most wonderful seasonings, soy sauce appears in almost every aspect of Japanese cooking. I love it and use it all the time, but for sushi, it should be used sparingly – for dipping and not for drowning the food. There is an art to dipping a piece of hand-formed sushi into soy sauce without it disintegrating and leaving grains of rice floating in the dish (see below). Whether you are using chopsticks or your fingers, try to eat hand-formed sushi in one mouthful;

it is considered impolite to bite a piece of sushi in half and then put the remaining half back on your plate.

When dipping a piece of rolled sushi, dip only a small corner of it in the soy sauce. Don't submerge the sushi as not only will it fall apart, but the rice will quickly absorb all the soy sauce and the delicate flavours of the roll will be totally overwhelmed. The same technique of immersing the corner only applies for dipping battleship sushi in soy sauce.

HOW TO DIP HAND-FORMED SUSHI

1 Pour a little soy sauce into a small dipping bowl. Tip the piece of sushi to one side on the plate and pick it up, holding it between your thumb and middle finger.

2 Turn your hand slightly to dip only the topping in the soy sauce. Pop the piece of sushi into your mouth upside down, so you taste the topping and soy first.

WASABI WISDOM

I have watched people dissolve an entire mound of wasabi paste in their soy sauce dipping dish and then proceed to drown a piece of sushi or sashimi in it. Up until now I have recommended that you eat according to your personal tastes and are not intimidated by convention, but this is where I draw the line. Wasabi is an essential accompaniment to sushi and sashimi, but it is intended to enhance the flavour of the food and should never be regarded as a proof of bravery.

If you like the taste and sensation of wasabi, dab a little extra wasabi paste on an individual piece of sushi or sashimi then dip it briefly in the soy sauce. This way, you can

A MOUND OF WASABI PASTE

savour the unique flavour of the fish and yet still enjoy the essence of the wasabi and soy sauce. At a sushi bar, ask the chef to apply a little more wasabi to your sushi and he will be more than happy to oblige.

PICKLED GINGER

Sushi is served with a little heap of thinly sliced pink pickled ginger. It is intended as a palate cleanser and should be eaten a slice at a time in between different flavours of sushi. Although pickled ginger's refreshing taste is rather addictive for some people, it is meant as an accompaniment to sushi or sashimi, not as a side salad.

PALATE-CLEANSING GINGER

Offer pickled ginger in a shared dish for people to help themselves

WHAT TO DRINK WITH SUSHI
tea, beer, sake, and wine

The Japanese drink whatever they wish with their meal, and good sushi restaurants and bars offer a wide range of beverages. The most traditional drinks to enjoy are probably hot green tea or sake (Japanese rice wine), but Japanese beer is also a good option. Sushi has become such an international food that both red and white wine are also popular choices.

GREEN TEA

A cup of hot green tea, known as *agari*, is not only refreshing but cleanses the palate during a sushi meal. It is a gentle digestive aid and contains vitamins A, B, and C.

BEER

Beer has a crisp, refreshing quality that goes well with sushi and sashimi. Japanese beers, or *bīru*, tend to be closer in flavour to American and European lagers and are always served cold. There are many different Japanese beers available, but non-Japanese beers are also perfectly suitable for your meal.

SAKE

An alcoholic drink made from fermented rice, sake has a smooth, subtle flavour that perfectly complements Japanese food. It is quite potent, with an alcohol content of 15–20 per cent. There is a huge range on offer but, in general, sake types are named to describe how they were made. Sake is made from "polished", or milled, rice; the more the rice is polished, the purer its starch content becomes, and the more

COLD, CRISP JAPANESE BEER

refined the flavour of the finished sake will be. Sometimes a tiny amount of distilled alcohol is added to make the sake; this is different to sake made from fermented rice only, which is called *junmai* (literally "pure rice").

• *Junmaishu* is sake made from rice with at least 30 per cent of the kernel removed and no added distilled alcohol. It is generally slightly heavier and fuller-flavoured than other types of sake, and is more acidic. It goes well with a wide range of food.

• *Honjōzōshu* is sake made from rice with at least 30 per cent of the kernel removed and a little added distilled alcohol. It is usually lighter than *junmaishu* and can be drunk at room temperature or warmed.

• *Ginjōshu* is sake made from rice with at least 40 per cent of the kernel removed and a little added distilled alcohol. This sake has a layered, complex flavour that is light and fragrant.

• *Junmaiginjōshu* is the no-added-alcohol version of *ginjōshu*.

• *Daiginjōshu* is the most expensive sake. It is made from rice with at least 50 per cent of the kernel removed and a little added distilled alcohol. It is highly fragrant and even lighter than *ginjōshu*.

• *Junmaidaiginjōshu* is the no-added-alcohol version of *daiginjōshu*.

A balanced, medium-dry wine is a good choice to drink with sushi

WINE

While I generally recommend that you choose whatever wine you like drinking, bear in mind that your choice of wine should not be so dry that it clashes with the fish, and nor should it be so sweet that it swamps the delicate flavours. Riesling is a good pairing for sushi, as is champagne. Full-bodied red wine can complement classic *toro*, or fatty tuna, and other oily fish very well, as the tannins in the wine can make oily fish taste even more buttery.

MEDIUM-DRY WHITE WINE

15

BASICS

UTENSILS
dōgu

If you already have a reasonably **well-equipped** kitchen, you can make sushi without having to add a whole range of new specialist equipment. The aim of this book is to **get you started** making sushi at home, so I have kept the list to just a few pieces of **essential equipment**, and some additional **specialist items** you may wish to add later.

In most cases, you can **improvise** the specialist equipment used for making sushi, so wherever possible I advise which Western kitchen utensils can be used as **alternatives**. For a keen cook, however, it's always a pleasure adding to your kitchen equipment, and most of the **traditional** equipment is **inexpensive** and has the advantage of having been designed specifically for sushi preparation. Thanks to the **ever-increasing popularity** of sushi, most of the equipment you need to prepare it can be found in large department stores, **Japanese or Asian supermarkets**, or online.

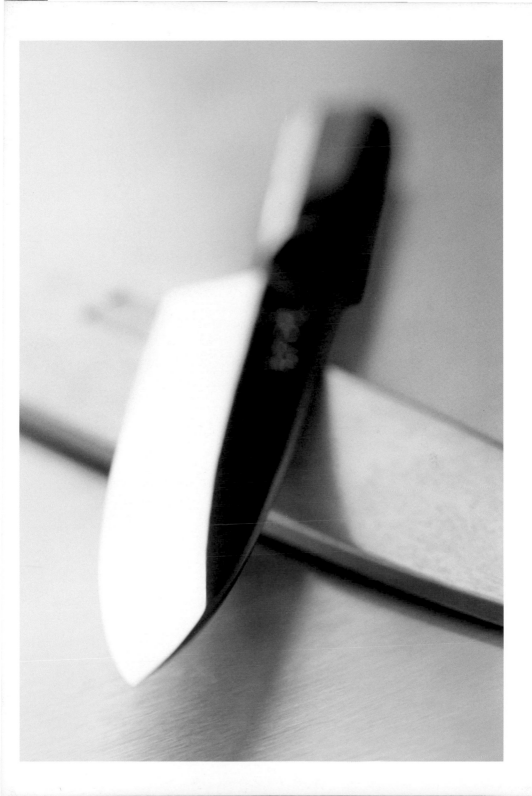

ESSENTIAL EQUIPMENT
dōgu

These utensils will make sushi preparation easier and are available from kitchen sections in large department stores. A set of good knives is a sound investment for any kitchen, but if you cannot get Japanese knives use the sharpest, best-quality knives you can for ingredient preparation. The only specialist item for which there is no substitute, however, is a bamboo rolling mat.

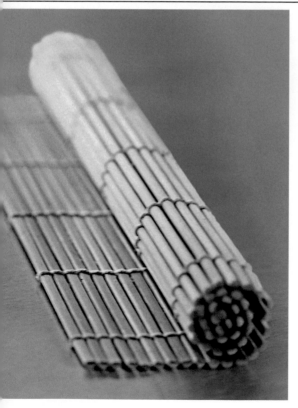

BAMBOO ROLLING MAT
makisu

A specialist rolling mat is essential for making rolled sushi. It is made of bamboo sticks woven together with cotton string and is square in shape, usually measuring around 24 x 24cm (10 x 10in). Although there is no suitable substitute, bamboo rolling mats are easily available, even in supermarkets, and are inexpensive.

After use, your bamboo rolling mat must be washed and cleaned with cold water (and a brush if necessary) without any detergent. Make sure to dry it completely before storing. Any moisture and traces of starch from rice left on it will result in it becoming mouldy. You may cover the mat with a sheet of cling film when making inside-out rolls to avoid rice grains getting stuck between the bamboo sticks. In Japanese kitchens, the mat is also used to drain vegetables and for shaping rolled omelettes.

KNIVES
hōchō

A sushi chef's knife is as precious to him as a sword to a samurai warrior. The ancient craft of Japanese sword making is still practised today, only it is used to forge kitchen knives made of superior quality carbon steel. These knives need to be properly looked after to maintain their hair-splitting sharpness. They should be sharpened by hand with a whetstone, never with a steel knife sharpener or grinding wheel.

You are more likely to injure yourself with a blunt knife, so look after your knife and it will serve you well. Don't put it in the dishwasher, wash it by hand. Don't store it in a drawer with other kitchen tools that might chip the blade. If you have a knife block, slide the knife into a slot on its back, not on the sharp blade.

If you cannot sharpen it yourself, have it done professionally; good kitchen shops should offer the service.

Japanese knives are sharpened on one side of the blade, the cutting edge, which is always on the right side. If you are left-handed, you will need a specially adapted left-handed knife. A sushi chef normally has at least three different types of knife (pictured from left to right):

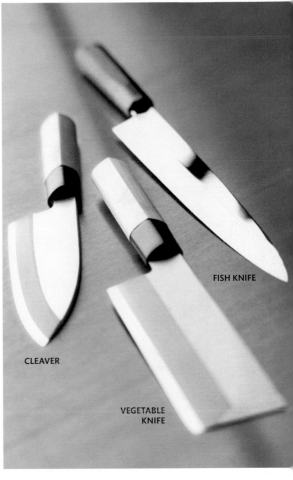

FISH KNIFE

CLEAVER

VEGETABLE KNIFE

CLEAVER
deba bōchō

This knife's heavy, curved blade is ideal for cutting through fish bones.

VEGETABLE KNIFE
usuba bōchō

In the hands of a sushi chef, this knife peels, cuts, and chops faster and finer than a food processor. Its blade is straight and thinner than that of other knives, which makes it suitable for delicate work.

FISH KNIFE
yanagi bōchō

This long, slender blade is used for slicing fish fillets, cutting sushi rolls, and making decorative garnishes.

ADDITIONAL EQUIPMENT
for making sushi

There are three more specialist items you may wish to add to your sushi-making equipment. While they are not essential – each can be improvised with your existing Western kitchen equipment – having them, especially a wooden rice tub, will make the job much easier.

WOODEN RICE TUB
hangiri or handai

Made of cypress wood and bound with copper wire, this broad, flat-bottomed, low-sided tub is specially designed for preparing sushi rice. Its shape speeds the cooling process and makes it easier to fold in the sushi vinegar mixture. The wood absorbs the excess moisture and helps give the rice its characteristic glossiness. It needs soaking in cold water before use to prevent rice from sticking to it. After use, wash it well in cold water without any detergent, and use a brush or the coarse side of a washing-up sponge to remove any rice starch. Dry it completely, away from direct sunlight, before storing in a cool, dark place. A low-sided, non-metallic tub or salad bowl makes a good substitute.

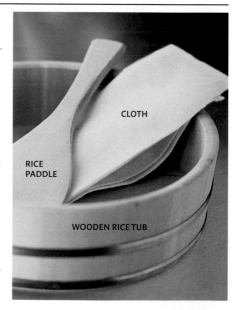

CLOTH

RICE PADDLE

WOODEN RICE TUB

RICE PADDLE
shamoji

A flat, round-shaped paddle is traditionally used to serve rice and stir in sushi vinegar, and is made of bamboo or wood. Soak it in cold water before use to stop rice sticking to it. Alternatively, use a spatula.

CLOTH
fukin

Simple but very useful – damp cotton or linen cloths are used to clean fish, utensils, or to wipe the chef's hands. You can also use them to shape *temari* sushi balls (see pp.236–39) instead of using cling film.

JAPANESE SQUARE OMELETTE PAN
tamagoyaki-ki

There are two types of Japanese omelette pan available: square copper pans, usually measuring 18 x 18cm (7 x 7in), and rectangular non-stick pans, usually measuring 12 x 18cm (5 x 7in). The copper ones are expensive and used by professionals, while the non-stick ones are less costly and sufficient for home use. Although it is possible to make a rolled omelette by using a conventional round pan of a similar size and simply trimming off the round edges on both ends of the finished omelette, having a square pan makes it easier and quicker to achieve the desired result.

PRESSED SUSHI MOULD
oshibako

Traditionally made from cypress wood, which is the same wood usually used for the sushi counter, pressed sushi moulds have removable bottoms and lids. They come in various sizes and shapes, but are commonly square or rectangular. To prevent the rice from sticking, they need to be soaked in cold water before use and the excess water wiped away with a damp cloth. Care for it in the same way as the rice tub (see opposite). Good substitutes for a sushi mould would be a small cooking ring, a plastic box lined with cling film, or a springform cake tin – you can make a sushi "cake" and cut it into individual portions.

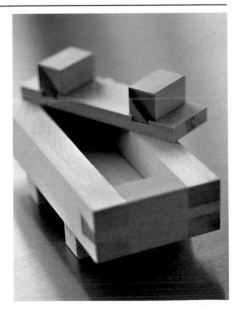

INGREDIENTS

zairyō

Sushi's rising popularity has made it much easier to find essential ingredients such as Japanese-style **short grain rice**, **rice vinegar**, and **soy sauces** in larger supermarkets.

Ingredients such as dried gourd (*kampyō*) and shiitake mushrooms need to be reconstituted and flavoured in a **seasoned broth** before use. You need to set aside **time** to do this, but they can be **prepared in advance** and kept in an airtight container placed in the refrigerator for up to three days. Most storecupboard ingredients have **long shelf lives** if kept in the right conditions, so stock up and all you'll need to shop for whenever making sushi are **fresh fish and vegetables**.

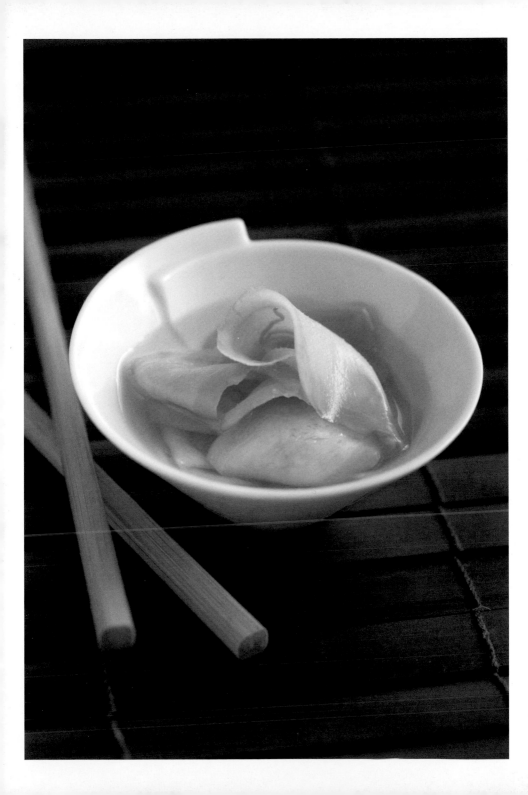

STORECUPBOARD ESSENTIALS

Many of the essential ingredients needed for making sushi at home –
Japanese-style rice, soy sauce, and wasabi, for example – are available
in large supermarkets these days. More specialist sushi ingredients are
easy to find in Japanese food shops and most have long shelf lives.
I have suggested alternatives wherever possible.

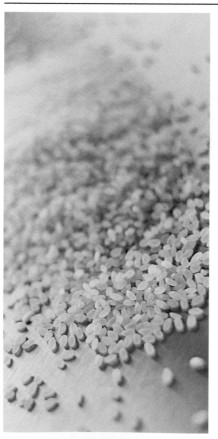

SHORT GRAIN JAPANESE RICE

JAPANESE-STYLE RICE
kome

Japanese-style short grain rice is essential
for sushi. Its high starch content absorbs a lot
of moisture, which gives it its characteristic
stickiness when cooked. Japanese rice is
harvested in the late autumn, and new crop
is labelled *shinnmai*, literally "new rice", and is
renowned for its delicate flavour. However,
for sushi, such moist, soft new rice is disliked
and top sushi restaurants go a long way to
secure the previous year's drier, harder grains.
Long grain rice, such as basmati or Thai
Jasmine rice, is not suitable for making
sushi as it does not possess the necessary
absorbency, nor does it become sticky.
Genuine Japanese-grown rice has become
easier to find in Japanese stores and via
internet retailers, but the USA also produces
excellent-quality Japanese-style rice.

DRIED SEAWEED
nori

Nori is made from different types of Porphyra algae that are washed and spread thinly to dry on mesh sheets. Choose nori that is dark and tightly grained; the thinner and greener, the more inferior the quality. Store it in an airtight bag or container in a dark place.

NORI SHEETS
These come in a standard size of 20.5 x 19cm (8 x 7in) and are usually sold in a pack of 10. The upper side (usually on show) is smooth and shiny, while the underside is coarse and grainy. Nori has a mild, aromatic flavour and a paper-like quality that allows it to be used as an edible wrapping material for various styles of sushi. To revive a stale, limp nori sheet, hold it 15cm (6in) above a gentle gas flame for a few minutes, or until it becomes crisp and the aroma returns.

PACKET OF NORI SHEETS

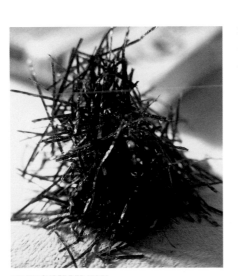

READY-SHREDDED NORI

SHREDDED NORI
Shredded nori makes a tasty and attractive garnish for scattered sushi. You can buy packets of ready-shredded nori sheets, but if you cannot find these, then stack a few nori sheets on top of each other and finely slice them using a sharp knife, or cut them using scissors. Avoid using a serrated knife to cut nori, which will tear the delicate sheets.

CONTINUED ▶

WASABI
wasabi

This green horseradish is also known as *namida*, meaning tears, as it is fiercely pungent. Wasabi should not be used to prove one's bravery, but eaten in very small quantities, it will enhance the flavour of the sushi. It is readily available as a powder and ready-mixed in tubes.

POWDERED WASABI
Widely available in supermarkets and Japanese shops, powdered wasabi has a long shelf life and retains its flavour well. Make a stiff paste by mixing 1 tsp wasabi powder with 1 tsp water. Leave to stand for 5–10 minutes before use to allow the flavours to develop. The paste can be moulded into decorative shapes and used as a garnish (see p.51).

▲ MIXING POWDERED WASABI
Reconstitute powdered wasabi with a little cold water and mix it thoroughly to make a paste. You can mould stiffer pastes into shapes.

READY-MIXED TUBES OF WASABI
Although convenient to use, once opened, the wasabi paste you can buy ready-mixed in tubes quickly loses its pungency and flavour. The texture of this paste is a little softer to make it easy to squeeze from the tube.

READY-MIXED WASABI PASTE

Wasabi should be used to enhance, not to overpower

SOY SAUCE
shōyu

This is arguably the most important seasoning in Japanese cooking. Made from fermented soybeans, wheat, and salt, there are different versions available. The dark variety is the most versatile and is used both in cooking and as a dipping sauce for sushi, while light soy sauce is used for cooking only. Tamari is also made from fermented soybeans, but it is wheat-free, thicker, and more fragrant. Strictly speaking, tamari is used for dipping. It can be a good option for those who are gluten intolerant, but always check the label first.

LIGHT SOY SAUCE   DARK SOY SAUCE   TAMARI

PICKLED GINGER
gari

Usually served on the corner of a sushi tray to accompany sushi, pink pickled ginger should be eaten a slice at a time. It cleanses the palate between mouthfuls and aids digestion. Although you can make your own, ready-prepared is normally of good quality. Once opened, it should be kept in the refrigerator.

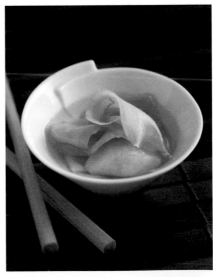

SLICES OF PICKLED GINGER

CONTINUED ▶

SU, OR RICE VINEGAR

RICE VINEGAR
su

Pale gold in colour, Japanese rice vinegar has a mild, slightly tart flavour and leaves a subtle aftertaste. It is an essential ingredient in sushi, not least because it is used to flavour the rice. Rice vinegar is a preservative and also has antibacterial properties. It is available in Japanese food shops and supermarkets, but cider vinegar or red wine vinegar diluted with a little water make adequate substitutes.

JAPANESE RICE WINE
sake

The national alcoholic drink of Japan, sake is one of the best accompaniments to sushi and can be drunk hot or cold. It is an important ingredient in cooking, where it is used to tenderize meat and fish, and to enhance flavour. Dry sherry is a good substitute. For cooking purposes, buy sake labelled as ryori sake, or inexpensive drinking sake.

RYORI SAKE FOR COOKING

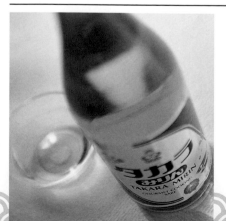

SWEET RICE WINE
mirin

Also known as sweet sake, mirin is used strictly for cooking. It adds gloss and creates a well-rounded depth of flavour. If it is unavailable, use 1 tsp sugar for 1 tbsp mirin. Store in a cool, dark place after opening.

MIRIN, OR SWEET SAKE

DRIED GOURD
kampyō

Kampyo is sold dried in long, thin strips. It is traditionally used as a filling for rolled sushi, chopped up as a topping for scattered sushi, and also makes a useful ribbon to tie parcels of stuffed sushi. It has a firm, almost chewy, texture and takes on the flavour of its seasonings. It is available from Japanese food shops. Before use, it needs to be reconstituted in a lightly seasoned broth (see below). Once prepared, kampyo will keep in the refrigerator in a sealed container for up to three days.

DRIED STRIPS OF KAMPYO

HOW TO PREPARE DRIED GOURD

1 Wash 30g (1oz) kampyo in cold water using a scrubbing action. Add 2 tbsp salt and rub in the water until soft. Rinse and soak in water for 2 hours or overnight (check packet instructions).

2 Drain, place in a saucepan with enough fresh water to cover, and simmer for 10–15 minutes. Add 500ml (17fl oz) dashi (see p.47), 2 tbsp sugar, and 2 tbsp soy sauce, bring to the boil, then simmer for 10 minutes, or until the kampyo is golden. Allow to cool in the stock before cutting to desired lengths.

CONTINUED ▶

DRIED SHIITAKE MUSHROOMS
shiitake

These intensely flavoured mushrooms are used as a filling in thick roll sushi and as a versatile topping for scattered, pressed, and hand-formed sushi. They will keep for up to six months in a cool, dry place. They need to be reconstituted and seasoned before use (see below), but when soaked, good-quality dried shiitake mushrooms are fleshy, plump, meaty tasting, and stronger in flavour than their fresh counterparts.

DRIED SHIITAKE MUSHROOM

HOW TO SEASON SHIITAKE MUSHROOMS

Soak 30g (1oz) dried shiitake mushrooms in 250ml (8fl oz) hot water for about 20 minutes. Drain, reserving the soaking liquid, and cut off and discard the stems. Add the mushrooms to 250ml (8fl oz) dashi (see p.47) and the reserved liquid in a saucepan, and cook over a gentle heat for about 30 minutes, or until the liquid has reduced by half. Add 1 tbsp mirin, then remove from heat and let cool in the liquid before using.

TOASTED SESAME SEEDS
iri goma

Both black and white sesame seeds are available ready-toasted from Japanese food shops, but their nutty flavour tends to fade. To revive their flavour, dry-toast them in a pan over a gentle heat for 1–2 minutes; keep them moving to prevent burning, which makes them bitter.

BLACK AND WHITE TOASTED SESAME SEEDS

KELP
konbu or kombu

Usually labelled "kombu" in the English-speaking world, this seaweed is one of the most important ingredients in Japanese cuisine, essential for making dashi stock (see p.47) as well as numerous dishes and preserves. There are 10 species of kombu found in the cold waters off the coast of Hokkaido island, in northern Japan. Once harvested in summer, it is dried on the beach in the sun, cut, and folded into manageable lengths. It contains a high level of natural monosodium glutamate – the key element of *umami*, the fifth taste. Do not wash it, but wipe it lightly with a clean, damp cloth before use. Its shelf life is almost indefinite if you keep it in a dry, dark cupboard.

SHEETS OF KOMBU

DRIED BONITO FLAKES

BONITO FLAKES
katsuo bushi

These wood shaving-like flakes are one of the two essential ingredients of dashi, or Japanese stock (the other is kombu). They are made from dried, smoked, and matured fillet of bonito fish (see pp.66–67) and are available in a ready-to-use shaved form. Bonito flakes have a characteristic deep, smoky taste and aroma, and can be used as a garnish or topping as well as for making dashi stock.

FRESH FLAVOURINGS

The following fresh ingredients are quintessentially Japanese – vegetables and herbs that have long been cultivated in the country and appear widely in its cuisine. For sushi and sashimi, each provides an important supporting role: *daikon* is a natural digestive aid for fish, *renkon* is used for its pretty appearance and crunchy texture, while *shiso* is both refreshing and decorative.

MOULI
daikon

This large white radish is available from Asian supermarkets. Its subtle yet pungent flavour makes it an ideal accompaniment to sushi and sashimi. It can be cut into decorative shapes or shredded (see p.49) and used as a garnish. It should be peeled and soaked in cold water before use. Daikon is 90 per cent water; fresh ones should feel weighty and look tight-skinned without any dark blemishes. Store in the refrigerator, wrapped in damp paper towels.

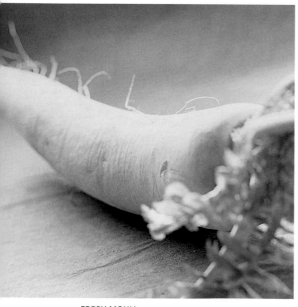

FRESH MOULI

HOW TO MAKE CHILLI DAIKON RELISH

This mildly spicy, fresh-tasting relish is the ideal accompaniment to Seared Beef Fillet and Red Onion Sushi (see pp.154–57). Peel 250g (9oz) daikon, soak briefly, then grate it into a bowl. Deseed and finely chop a small red chilli (or use 1 tsp chilli paste) and mix with the daikon.

LOTUS ROOT
renkon

The crunchy white root of the water lily, lotus root is white and honeycombed with holes. Highly seasonal, it is not always available fresh, even in Japan. Fresh lotus root is peeled and boiled in a mixture of water, sugar, and rice vinegar until soft. It is usually available tinned or pickled in vinegar from Japanese shops – this needs no further cooking.

PICKLED LOTUS ROOT

PERILLA LEAVES
shiso

This aromatic Japanese herb belongs to the mint family. It resembles the stinging nettle, with its fringed leaves, but has no sting. It has a distinctive, pungent flavour and is often used as an edible garnish for sushi platters and sashimi arrangements. Often sold in packets of 10 leaves in Japanese stores, choose ones with no dark blemishes. Keep the leaves in the refrigerator, wrapped in damp paper towels.

FRESH PERILLA LEAVES

BASIC RECIPES
kihon

The key to successful, stress-free sushi-making is **good organization**. The basic recipes that form the **components** of sushi are all straightforward and **easy to follow**, even if some of the ingredients may be new to you. If you plan ahead and prepare your rice, toppings, and garnishes **in readiness**, then making sushi is simply a matter of **assembly**.

At the base of it all is the vinegared **sushi rice**, *sushi meshi*. A young apprentice sushi chef can spend many years just watching his master from a respectful distance before being allowed to **prepare** sushi rice. But fear not, by following the **simple step-by-step** basic recipe and with a **little practice**, you will soon be making *sushi meshi* that is good enough to eat on its own. Remember that you can prepare the rice a few hours in **advance** and keep it covered with a clean, damp cloth until you are ready to use it.

As well as sushi rice, you will find out how to make **core recipes** such as Japanese omelette, **dashi stock**, garnishes, and some delicious soups that make the perfect start or end to a sushi meal.

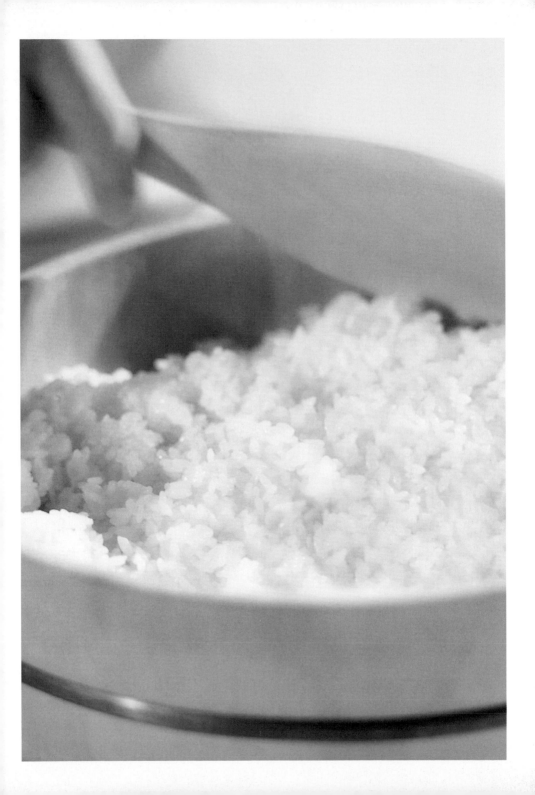

PREPARING SUSHI RICE

sushi meshi

Good sushi, whatever the style, always begins with good vinegared sushi rice. Cooked sushi rice is slightly harder in texture than average boiled rice because it is cooked with less water to allow some room for the addition of sushi vinegar. It is particularly important to wash and rinse the rice, then let the wet grains stand for at least 30 minutes before cooking to allow them to absorb some water.

SUSHI VINEGAR

Sushi vinegar is a blend of rice vinegar, sugar, and salt. It is the all-important, integral part of sushi, and gives otherwise plain rice a subtle sweet-and-sour taste and glossy sheen. There is no definitive recipe; the balance of sugar and salt can vary to suit different types of fillings or toppings – a slightly saltier vinegar mixture works well with strongly flavoured or oily fish, such as mackerel, tuna, or salmon, while milder ingredients, such as vegetables and white fish, call for a mixture that is a little sweeter.

There are endless formulas, and each sushi chef jealously guards his secret recipe, but a very general guide is to use 10 parts vinegar, 5 parts sugar, and 1 part salt. You could reduce the salt quantity if you wanted a sweeter mixture.

HOW TO PREPARE AND USE VINEGAR MIXTURE

Place the rice vinegar, sugar, and salt in a stainless steel saucepan and heat gently, stirring until the salt and sugar have dissolved. Don't let the mixture boil or it will spoil the flavour. Let it cool to room temperature before using it. You can make

up sushi vinegar mixture in advance; just store it in a glass container in the refrigerator and use it within 3 months. When adding premixed sushi vinegar to cooked rice, use approximately ½ tbsp vinegar mixture per 100g (3½oz) cooked rice.

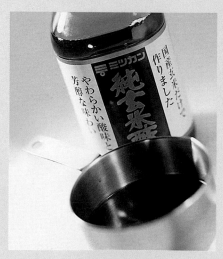

▲ **RICE VINEGAR**
When you blend it with sugar and salt, Japanese rice vinegar becomes sushi vinegar. It is this that creates the distinctive taste of sushi rice.

HOW TO MAKE

MAKES 600–660g (about 1lb 5oz) | **PREPARATION TIME** 1 hour 30 minutes

INGREDIENTS

300g (10oz) Japanese short grain rice

1 postcard-size piece of kombu (optional)

330ml (11fl oz) water for cooking

For the vinegar mixture

4 tbsp Japanese rice vinegar

2 tbsp sugar

½ tsp salt

METHOD

1 Rinse the rice in a sieve submerged in a large bowl of cold water. Wash it thoroughly and discard the milky water. Keep washing and changing the water until it is clear. Drain the water and leave the rice to stand in the sieve for 30 minutes. Meanwhile, prepare the vinegar mixture (see method opposite).

Kombu imparts a briny, savoury flavour known as umami

2 If using kombu, make a few cuts in it to help release its flavour as it cooks.

CONTINUED ▶

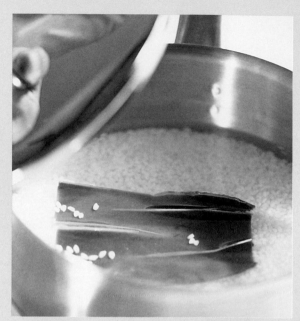

3 Put the washed rice and the 330ml (11fl oz) water in a heavy-bottomed saucepan with a tight-fitting lid. Add the kombu, if using, and let the water stand for 10–15 minutes before turning on the heat to medium. When the water comes to the boil, increase the heat to high and cook for a further 5 minutes. All the while, resist the temptation to lift the lid but listen for the sound of boiling and watch for escaping trails of steam instead.

4 Reduce the heat to low and simmer for a further 10 minutes, then turn off the heat. With the lid still on, let the rice stand and steam for 10–15 minutes. Meanwhile, soak the wooden rice tub, or *hangiri*, in cold water. If you are using an alternative, such as a wide flat dish or salad bowl, moisten it with a damp cloth. Lift the lid and discard the kombu.

5 Wipe the rice tub of excess water (no need to do this if you are using an alternative dish) and transfer the cooked rice to it. Sprinkle a little of the vinegar mixture over a spatula into the rice.

6 Spread the rice evenly in the tub. Slowly add a little more of the vinegar mixture, using a slicing action to coat the grains of rice and separate them.

7 Fan the rice gently to cool it. Continue to fold the vinegar mixture into the rice with the spatula until it begins to look glossy and has cooled to room temperature. If you are not using the sushi rice immediately, cover it with a clean, damp cloth to stop it drying out and set aside in a cool place – but never refrigerate. Refrigeration makes the rice hard and dry; the vinegar mixture preserves the rice. Use within the day.

SCRAMBLED EGGS

tamago soboro

The key to preparing Japanese scrambled eggs is to use cooking chopsticks to stir them. This action gives them their stringy appearance and keeps the pieces separate. Try them as a colourful topping for scattered sushi. Cooking chopsticks are extra long to protect hands from heat, but you can use a whisk instead.

SERVES 4 as sushi topping | **PREPARATION TIME** 10 minutes

INGREDIENTS

2 eggs, beaten | 1 tsp sugar | ½ tsp salt | 1 tsp vegetable oil

METHOD

1 Combine the eggs, sugar, and salt in a mixing bowl. Heat the oil in a frying pan over a medium heat. Pour the egg mixture into the pan, and cook stirring continuously with either chopsticks or a whisk.

2 When the egg begins to set, remove the pan from the heat but continue to stir to get a fluffy consistency.

THIN JAPANESE OMELETTE

usuyaki tamago

This thin omelette is folded and stuffed with sushi rice, or thinly sliced (known as *kinshi tamago* or "golden shreds") and used as a topping for scattered sushi. This should make one large omelette, using a frying pan about 24cm (9½in) in size.

MAKES 1 omelette | **PREPARATION TIME** 5 minutes

INGREDIENTS

1 tsp cornflour | 1 egg | 1 egg yolk | 1 tsp salt | 1 tsp vegetable oil

METHOD

1 Dissolve the cornflour in 1 tbsp of water. Add to a mixing bowl with all the remaining ingredients, except the oil, and mix well. Heat the oil in a pan over a medium heat (wipe away excess oil with a piece of folded kitchen paper), then pour in the egg mixture so that it coats the base of the pan thinly.

2 When the omelette begins to set, pick it up and turn it over with a chopstick or fork to cook the other side. Don't allow the omelette to crisp or overcook – it should remain a golden yellow colour.

3 Remove from the pan and transfer to a plate lined with kitchen paper. Either cut the round edges off the omelette for omelette parcels, or roll up and cut into fine shreds to use as a topping.

ROLLED JAPANESE OMELETTE

dashi maki tamago

Some sushi connoisseurs suggest that you begin your meal with a piece of hand-formed sushi topped with rolled Japanese omelette in order to test a sushi bar's rice and vinegar mix. The omelette is slightly sweet in flavour and succulently moist. It's best to use a square Japanese omelette pan (see p.23), but you can use a round pan and trim the round ends off the omelette. Once prepared, it keeps for a day wrapped in cling film and refrigerated.

MAKES 1 omelette | **PREPARATION TIME** 20 minutes

INGREDIENTS

6 eggs, beaten

125ml (4fl oz) dashi stock (p.47)

2 tbsp sugar

1 tsp salt

1 tbsp sake (optional)

1 tbsp mirin (optional)

1 tbsp vegetable oil for frying

METHOD

1 Combine the eggs and all the remaining ingredients, except the oil, in a mixing bowl. Heat the oil in a square omelette pan; wipe away excess oil with a piece of folded kitchen paper. Drop a small amount of egg mixture into the pan to test the temperature. If it sizzles, the pan is hot enough. Ladle one-third of the mixture into the pan, so that the base is thinly covered.

2 Cook over a medium heat until the surface begins to set and the edges begin to crisp.

3 Fold the omelette towards you in quarter sections using either chopsticks or a fork.

4 Push the folded omelette to the far end of the pan.

CONTINUED ▶

5 Add a little more oil to the exposed surface of the pan. Ladle in enough egg mixture to coat the base of the pan. Gently lift the folded omelette to allow the egg mixture to cover the entire base of the pan.

6 When the egg begins to set, fold it towards you in quarters, with the first roll at the centre.

7 Shape the omelette roll by gently pushing it against the side of the pan. Repeat the process until all the egg mixture is finished. Remove from the heat and set aside to cool before cutting.

MAKING JAPANESE STOCK
dashi

Dashi is the basic Japanese stock, used not only in soups (see pp.52–55) but also in many dishes such as salads, stews, and even rolled Japanese omelette. Unlike Western stock or bouillon, making dashi is relatively quick. For a vegetarian version, omit the bonito flakes and double the quantity of kombu.

MAKES 1 litre (1¾ pints) | **PREPARATION TIME** 20 minutes

INGREDIENTS
1 postcard-size piece of kombu | 1 litre (1¾ pints) water | 10g (⅓oz) bonito fish flakes

METHOD

1 Make some incisions in the kombu to help release more flavour. Put the water in a saucepan, add the kombu, and let it stand for 10 minutes before slowly bringing to the boil over a medium heat. Just before boiling point, remove the kombu and discard. Add the bonito flakes, but do not stir. Bring back to the boil, then immediately turn off the heat.

2 Let the bonito flakes settle, then strain the finished dashi stock through a muslin-lined sieve. Use the dashi within the same day of making it.

GARNISHES AND DECORATIONS
tsuma / kazari

It's not enough for sushi simply to taste delicious – take care over presentation as well. Carrot, daikon, and cucumber can be cut into flowers or shredded, and clever knife work can transform a cucumber into a pine branch to decorate sushi and soups. Wasabi leaves add an artistic touch to sushi and sashimi arrangements.

PREPARATION TIME about 5 minutes per decoration

EQUIPMENT
flower-shaped vegetable cutter

MAKING CARROT FLOWERS

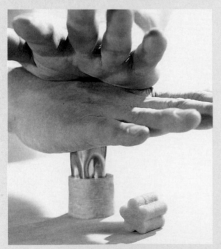

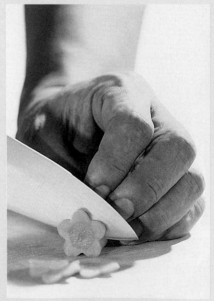

1 Peel a small to medium-sized carrot and cut it into 4cm (1¾in) lengths. Place a piece of carrot on its end on a stable chopping board and use a vegetable cutter to cut it into flower-shaped pieces. Repeat with the remaining pieces.

2 Slice the carrot pieces as thinly as possible to make small flowers.

SHREDDING CUCUMBER

1 Take a 6cm (2½in) piece of cucumber and slice about 1cm (½in) off lengthways to give a flat edge. Cut several very thin slices, stopping when you reach the seeded core. Rotate the cucumber and do the same on the other side.

2 Place the slices on top of each other and slice thinly to give a shredded effect. Soak in water for 10 minutes, then use as a garnish. You can shred daikon in the same way, also soaking it for 10 minutes before using it.

MAKING AN EXPERT CUCUMBER GARNISH

1 Insert a knife blade under the skin of a 10cm (4in) length of cucumber. Turn the cucumber against the knife to produce a long, thin sheet.

2 Cut the cucumber sheet into several equal-sized pieces, pile on top of each other, and slice carefully into fine strands. Soak in water for 10 minutes, then use as a garnish.

CONTINUED ▶

MAKING A CUCUMBER PINE BRANCH

1 Cut a 7.5cm (3in) long piece of cucumber in half and cut off the skin on the sides. Make a series of lengthways cuts about 2–3mm (⅛in) apart, leaving a 1cm (½in) base at the end.

2 Slice the piece of cucumber in half lengthways.

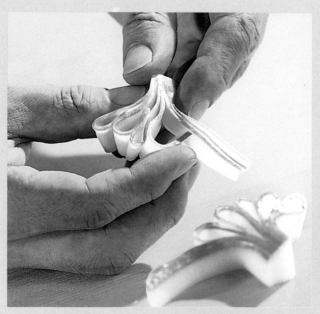

3 Carefully fold in each of the cut strips of cucumber, tucking each one into the gap between itself and the next strip. Leave the last strip of cucumber unfolded.

MAKING A WASABI LEAF

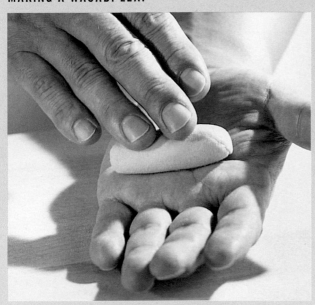

1 To make 4 leaves, mix 4 tbsp wasabi powder with 4 tsp water to make a smooth paste. Take a quarter of the mixture and work it into a cylindrical shape by rolling it in the palm of your hand.

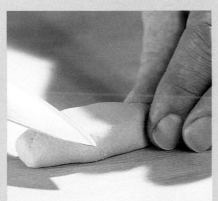

2 Place the cylinder on a chopping board and pinch one end to make a stem. Flatten the cylinder with the flat part of a knife blade and mould into a leaf shape with your fingers. Smooth over any cracks with a damp knife blade, if necessary.

3 Use a knife to score a stem and the veins of a leaf on to the wasabi. Repeat the process to make the remaining leaves.

CLEAR SOUP WITH EGG AND SHIITAKE MUSHROOMS

The egg in this soup separates into strands and provides a soft, delicate contrast to the earthy flavour of the shiitake mushrooms.

SERVES 4 | **PREPARATION TIME** 25 minutes

INGREDIENTS

1 quantity dashi stock (p.47)

2 eggs, beaten

4 fresh shiitake mushrooms, stems removed

1 tbsp light soy sauce

1 tbsp sake

salt

fresh coriander, to garnish

METHOD

1 Heat the dashi stock in a small saucepan until it reaches boiling point, then remove from the heat.

2 Add the beaten egg, pouring it through a wire sieve to create strands. Use a whisk to make gentle, circular waves in the pan to separate the strands. Don't whisk the soup.

3 Add the mushroom caps and season with the soy sauce, sake, and salt to taste. Bring back to the boil over a low heat, then immediately remove from the heat.

4 Ladle the soup into serving bowls, garnish with a sprig of coriander, and serve.

CLEAR SOUP WITH WHITE FISH

Use any white fish such as red snapper, sole, or sea bass for this soup. Leaving the skin on the fish helps to keep its shape and also adds a decorative touch.

SERVES 4 | **PREPARATION TIME** 20 minutes

INGREDIENTS

1 quantity dashi stock (p.47)

120g (4oz) white fish fillets such as red snapper, sole, or sea bass, cut into 8 pieces

1 tbsp light soy sauce

1 tbsp mirin

salt

4 spring onions, finely sliced

METHOD

1 Place the dashi stock and fish in a small saucepan over a medium heat. Just before it reaches boiling point, add the soy sauce, mirin, and salt to taste.

2 Bring the soup back to the boil, then immediately remove the saucepan from the heat.

3 Put two pieces of fish skin-side up in each serving bowl. Gently ladle the soup over the fish, garnish with the spring onion slices, and serve.

Back: Clear soup with egg and shiitake mushrooms   **Front:** Clear soup with white fish

CLAM MISO SOUP

asari miso shiru

This classic miso soup is easy to prepare as the cooking water is used for the broth. The colour of miso varies, but generally the darker it is, the saltier it tastes.

SERVES 4 | **PREPARATION TIME** 20 minutes

INGREDIENTS

4 tbsp miso paste

1 quantity dashi stock (p.47)

20 clams (p.133), washed thoroughly

salt

2 spring onions, finely sliced

METHOD

1 Dissolve the miso paste in a little hot water and add to a saucepan with the dashi stock and clams. Bring gently to the boil, skimming any residue from the surface, then remove from the heat and put the lid on the saucepan.

2 Leave the lid on the saucepan for 1–2 minutes until the clams have opened; discard any clams that have not opened. Season the soup with salt to taste.

3 Ladle the soup into individual bowls, garnish with the spring onion slices, and serve.

SPRING MISO SOUP

I use purple sprouting broccoli in this soup, but mangetout or asparagus also work well. Use light miso paste to match the delicate flavour of the vegetables.

SERVES 4 | **PREPARATION TIME** 20 minutes

INGREDIENTS

4 tbsp light miso paste

1 quantity dashi stock (p.47)

250g (9oz) purple sprouting broccoli

salt

60g (2oz) firm tofu, cut into 1cm (½in) cubes

1 tbsp toasted sesame seeds, to garnish (optional)

METHOD

1 Dissolve the miso paste in a little hot water and add to a saucepan with the dashi stock and broccoli. Bring to the boil over a gentle heat, then reduce the heat and simmer for 3 minutes. Season with salt to taste.

2 Add the cubed tofu and bring back to the boil, then remove from the heat.

3 Ladle the soup into individual bowls, garnish with the toasted sesame seeds, if using, and serve.

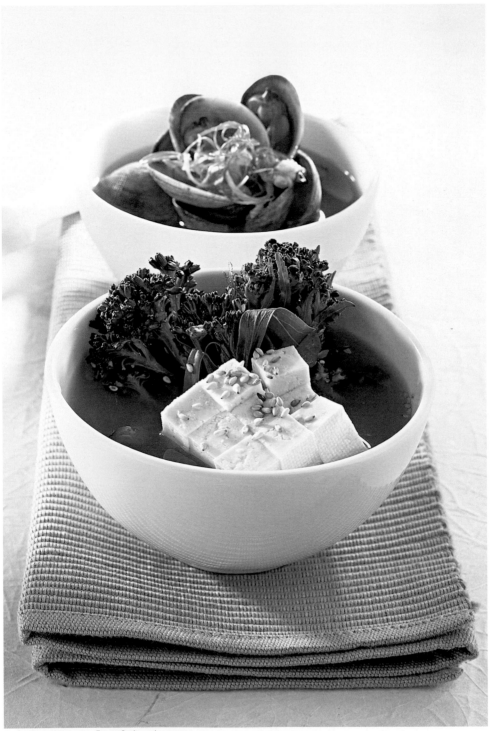

Back: Clam miso soup   **Front:** Spring miso soup

FISH, SHELLFISH, AND ROE

SEAFOOD SAFETY AND SUSTAINABILITY
making responsible choices

One of the best things you can do as a home sushi cook is to become informed about both the freshness and the sustainability of the seafood you are buying. Sourcing seafood to eat raw can be tricky, as there are no legal definitions of "sushi grade" and "sashimi grade". At the same time, the sustainability status of individual fish and shellfish changes over time, so it's important to know the issues and keep up to date with the latest recommendations. Ask where your seafood comes from, how it was caught, and how it was stored and prepared, to help you to make choices you are satisfied with.

JUDGING QUALITY

Although "sushi grade" and "sashimi grade" are not legally regulated terms, fishmongers sometimes use these labels for their freshest fish. However, fresh fish isn't always safe to eat raw – some fish that is sold for sushi and sashimi is frozen to kill bacteria and parasites. Guidelines from UK, EU, and US governing bodies specify that these fish should be frozen to not more than -20°C (-4°F), although some suppliers use the Japanese "superfreezing" technique of freezing to -60°C (-76°F) to retain maximum quality.

If in doubt, find a reliable and reputable fishmonger or fish market and ask when and where the fish was caught – it should be within 48 hours – and look to see if the fish is iced and stored properly, not sitting in melting water. Ask whether the fish has undergone freezing treatments and is safe to eat raw. Don't be afraid to get up close and inspect the fish for freshness – use your eyes, nose, and sense of touch to judge the quality (see p.60 and p.104 for tips).

▲ **FRESHLY CAUGHT FISH**
As soon as they are caught, fish are chilled, vacuum packed, or frozen on the vessel.

▲ SELECTIVE NET
This net has different-sized holes so that only the target species is caught and others can escape.

Fish for raw consumption should also be stored and handled separately from other fish to prevent cross-contamination. If you ask your fishmonger to fillet and skin your fish, make sure he or she uses a clean chopping board and knife.

There are also online suppliers that specialize in seafood for sushi and sashimi, but as always, make sure you understand how your fish has been handled.

CHOOSING SUSTAINABLE SEAFOOD

Several factors can affect sustainability, and the situation continually evolves.

Fish species decline when they are "overfished", or removed from the water at a greater rate than the time they need to grow and reproduce. Large, slow-growing species, such as tuna and halibut, are most vulnerable to overfishing. Choose fish from well-managed fisheries, and avoid small, immature fish that are caught before they've had a chance to reproduce.

Some fishing methods can cause a lot of damage to the seabed, such as beam trawls, bottom trawls, and dredges. Other methods, such as pelagic longlines, can capture vulnerable non-target species (known as "bycatch"), such as sea birds, turtles, and dolphins.

Aquaculture, or fish farming, can be an issue when the fish are kept in open sea pens, thus polluting the surrounding water. Sometimes the fish feed used is also not sustainable. However, farming is a good option for many shellfish, which don't require additional feed.

Organizations such as the Marine Stewardship Council certify sustainable fisheries, so look for their mark. Also refer to conservation groups, such as the UK's Marine Conservation Society, that provide guides to sustainable seafood.

ROUND FISH AND FLATFISH
sakana

The following pages will help you to **identify fish** that are suitable for sushi and sashimi and help you to buy them **sustainably**, in their **freshest** state, and **in season** (when they will be better in flavour, texture, and price). You will also learn which cuts of fish to choose and the correct way to **prepare them**.

I cannot stress enough the importance of buying the freshest fish possible for sushi and sashimi. A **whole fish** offers more clues to its freshness than a small cut piece, and although it is not always practical to buy a whole fish, it is often possible to see it before it is filleted. Check the following when buying fish:

- **The eyes** – should be clear, bright and plump, not cloudy and sunken.
- **The gills** – should be a bright pink or red colour, not a dark, murky red.
- **The body** – press it gently; it should feel firm and springy, not spongy and sticky. It should have undamaged fins and tail.
- **The smell** – fresh fish smells clean and fresh from the sea, not unpleasantly fishy.

When buying a fillet, look for one that is bright in colour, not dull or darkened, and without pearly or rainbow-like discolouration. Make friends with your fishmonger – he or she should be happy to answer your questions.

HORSE MACKEREL
aji

For the Japanese, horse mackerel (also called scad or jack mackerel) is one of the most popular *hikari mono*, or "shiny things", a term that refers to small oily fish with shiny silver/blue skin. It is inexpensive, available year-round, and has a simple yet satisfying taste. However, outside Japan, its bony skeleton, sharp spines, and strong flavour make it an acquired taste. Horse mackerel is best served in *nigiri zushi* as it spoils quickly and therefore must be prepared skillfully at speed; it is one for the experienced sushi chef.

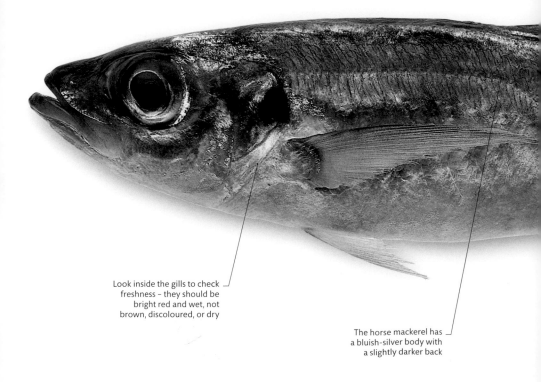

Look inside the gills to check freshness – they should be bright red and wet, not brown, discoloured, or dry

The horse mackerel has a bluish-silver body with a slightly darker back

Horse mackerel fillets

Like other *hikari mono* used in sushi, horse mackerel is served with the skin intact. It is milder in flavour than mackerel.

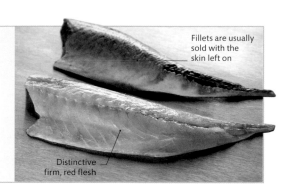

Fillets are usually sold with the skin left on

Distinctive firm, red flesh

The sharp, bony plates on the side of the horse mackerel's tail must be removed before eating

AVAILABILITY

There are 13 varieties of horse mackerel widely distributed in shallow waters around the world. Although they are available all year round, horse mackerel are at their best at certain times of the year: in Australia and Japan they are best in winter; in North America, along the east coast, they reach their prime during spring and summer; and in Europe during summer and autumn.

SUSTAINABILITY

Stock levels are unknown and unmanaged, so eat this fish only occasionally. Choose ones caught using lift nets as these fisheries have lower levels of bycatch. Avoid immature fish; mature horse mackerel are about 25cm (10in) long.

HERRING AND SARDINE
nishin / iwashi

Herring and sardines are closely related; there are some 180 varieties found across the world. Both of these distinctively flavoured fish are classified as *hikari mono*, or "shiny things" by the Japanese. However, like *aji* (see p.62), they are used in *nigiri zushi* only because they spoil very quickly and need expert preparation. In Japan, herring are highly valued for their roes, which are known as *kazunoko*, or "yellow diamonds".

HERRING

Herring and sardine fillets

Herring and sardines need to have their scales removed, but the fillets are served with the skin intact.

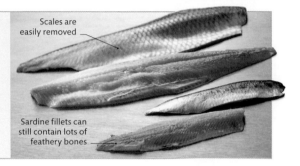

Scales are easily removed

Sardine fillets can still contain lots of feathery bones

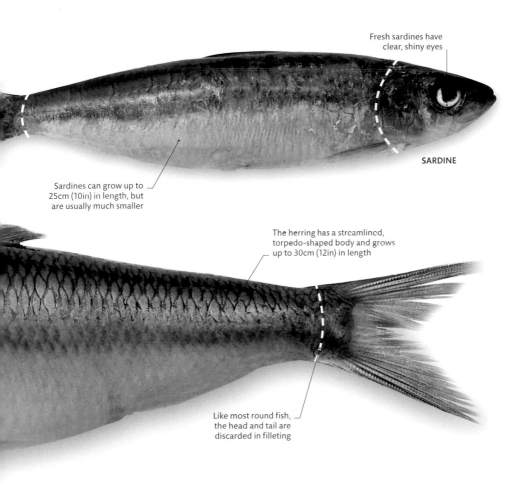

Fresh sardines have clear, shiny eyes

SARDINE

Sardines can grow up to 25cm (10in) in length, but are usually much smaller

The herring has a streamlined, torpedo-shaped body and grows up to 30cm (12in) in length

Like most round fish, the head and tail are discarded in filleting

AVAILABILITY

Sardines are commercially important in North America and are available all year round, but are not at their best during summer. Herring are available all year round in Europe, but are best from May to September. They are in season between December and February on the Pacific coast of North America, when they produce herring roe, and between winter and spring on the Atlantic coast.

SUSTAINABILITY

Herring is a good choice – its stocks are resilient, although some are in decline. Sardines are overfished in the Mediterranean region, so choose Pacific or North-east Atlantic sardines if possible. Both fish are caught using fairly low-impact methods.

BONITO
katsuo

Also known as skipjack tuna, bonito is a medium-sized fish related to tuna and belongs to the wider mackerel family. It is one of the fastest swimmers in the sea and is traditionally fished with a single rod rather than a large trawling net, which might damage its flesh. Bonito features in nearly every aspect of Japanese cuisine. It is eaten in sushi and marinated or lightly grilled as sashimi. Dried and shaved, it is used to make dashi, the basic Japanese stock. Bonito is often served with grated ginger, which complements its distinctive full, rich flavour.

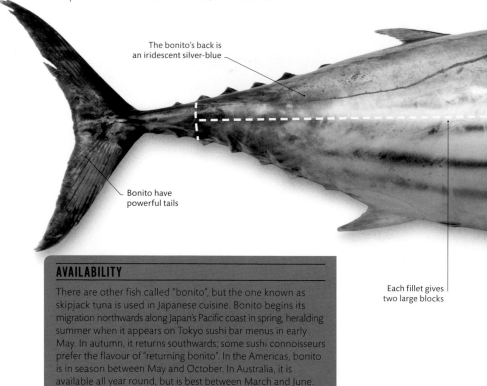

The bonito's back is an iridescent silver-blue

Bonito have powerful tails

Each fillet gives two large blocks

AVAILABILITY

There are other fish called "bonito", but the one known as skipjack tuna is used in Japanese cuisine. Bonito begins its migration northwards along Japan's Pacific coast in spring, heralding summer when it appears on Tokyo sushi bar menus in early May. In autumn, it returns southwards; some sushi connoisseurs prefer the flavour of "returning bonito". In the Americas, bonito is in season between May and October. In Australia, it is available all year round, but is best between March and June.

Bonito fillets

For sushi and sashimi, the skin is usually left on. The most popular method of serving it is *tataki* – lightly grilled then plunged into iced water to halt cooking and firm up the flesh.

Rosy-coloured flesh

Cuts from the back are more meaty than those from the belly

The large blocks are cut to make smaller pieces

SUSTAINABILITY

Bonito is less vulnerable to overfishing than other types of tuna. Those caught using troll or pole are the most sustainable. However, avoid purse seine fisheries using fishing aggregation devices (FADs), which attract a lot of vulnerable bycatch.

TUNA

maguro

Found in temperate and tropical oceans, tuna is a fast-swimming, migratory fish. It is related to the mackerel but is much larger – one species can grow to 4.3m (14ft) long and weigh up to 800kg (1,800lb). Its rich, red flesh is considered a delicacy and the fatty belly is the most prized cut. However, high demand has led to overfishing and, since tuna takes years to mature, its populations struggle to recover. Almost all tuna species are in decline, but bluefin tuna (*kuromaguro*) and bigeye tuna (*mebachi*) are near extinction and should be avoided.

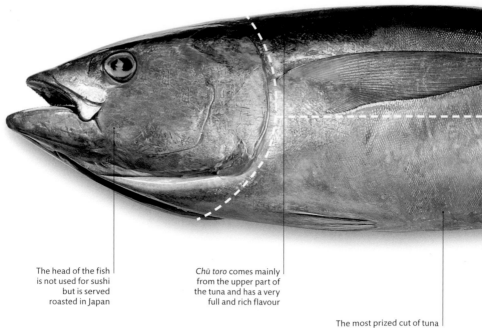

The head of the fish is not used for sushi but is served roasted in Japan

Chū toro comes mainly from the upper part of the tuna and has a very full and rich flavour

The most prized cut of tuna comes from the belly; *ō toro* is light pink, marbled with fat, and melts in the mouth

Tuna steaks

You are most likely to buy tuna in steak form. Choose a piece that is bright red in colour – not dark or greyish-brown. It should be moist but not wet looking. Lines of sinew should be evenly spaced.

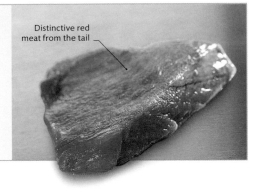

Distinctive red meat from the tail

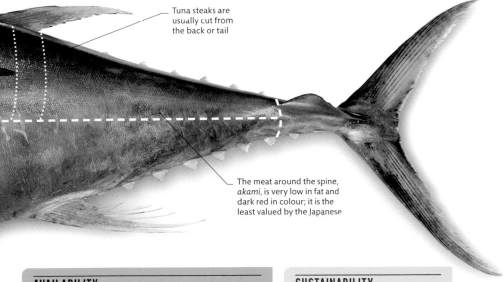

Tuna steaks are usually cut from the back or tail

The meat around the spine, *akami*, is very low in fat and dark red in colour; it is the least valued by the Japanese

AVAILABILITY

As it is a highly migratory fish, tuna is available all year round in various parts of the world, but is generally best in the cooler months. Albacore tuna (*binnaga*) is a smaller variety of tuna with paler flesh. Most are caught in the Pacific from June to October. Yellowfin tuna (*kihada*) is a smaller species and has a bright red-pink colour. It is found in the Western and Central Pacific region and the Indian ocean.

SUSTAINABILITY

Eat tuna only occasionally and choose certified fisheries. Many stocks are overfished and some fishing methods can cause damage. Albacore and yellowfin tuna are good choices. Avoid the traditional bluefin and bigeye tuna, which are both endangered.

MACKEREL

saba

Mackerel is arguably one of the healthiest, most sustainable, and tastiest fish available. It is found all over the world in temperate and tropical waters. Like other oily fish, its rich flesh contains high levels of omega-3 fatty acids, which are essential fats that help protect against heart disease and stroke. However, mackerel loses its freshness and nutrients quickly if it is not refrigerated as soon as it is caught. Therefore, traditionally, it is rarely eaten raw but is served cooked or semi-cured. *Battera* pressed sushi (see pp.182–85) is the most famous example.

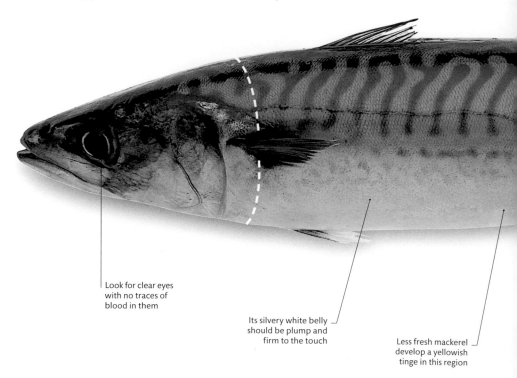

Look for clear eyes with no traces of blood in them

Its silvery white belly should be plump and firm to the touch

Less fresh mackerel develop a yellowish tinge in this region

Mackerel fillets

Intensely flavoured, mackerel is high in protein and rich in beneficial oils. You can buy mackerel fillets, or fillet the whole fish yourself (see pp.80–83).

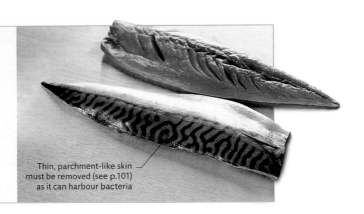

Thin, parchment-like skin must be removed (see p.101) as it can harbour bacteria

The mackerel has a shiny, blue-green coloured back with distinctive dark tabby markings

AVAILABILITY

There are three varieties of mackerel widely distributed all over the world: Pacific mackerel, Atlantic mackerel, and spotted mackerel, which are found in Australia, New Zealand, and the Hawaiian Islands. Available throughout the year, mackerel are in season from February to June in Europe, from summer to autumn in North America, and in the winter in Australia and New Zealand.

SUSTAINABILITY

Mackerel is a good choice as it reproduces quickly, which makes it relatively resilient. Choose fish caught from local, certified fisheries using ringnets, gillnets, drift nets, and handlines to ensure the least bycatch and environmental damage.

SALMON

sake

Most salmon species are anadromous: they are born in fresh water but then migrate to the open sea to grow to maturity before returning to their birthplace to spawn. In the wild, they feed on fish and crustaceans that give the flesh its distinctive colour. Salmon is native to the cool waters of the northern hemisphere, but is now farmed in many other parts of the world. It has become one of the most popular and recognizable raw sushi ingredients in the West, but in Japan this fish was traditionally salt-cured.

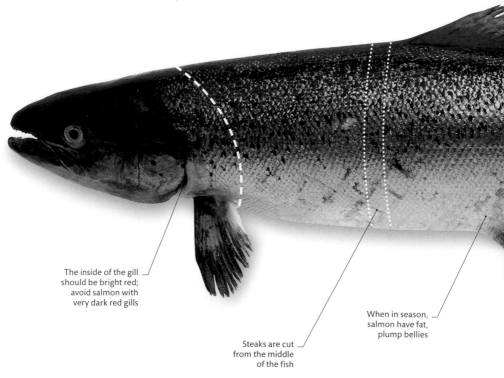

The inside of the gill should be bright red; avoid salmon with very dark red gills

Steaks are cut from the middle of the fish

When in season, salmon have fat, plump bellies

Steaks and fillets

Both of these cuts are readily available. Fillets may be more expensive, but they are a better shape for sushi (see p.96).

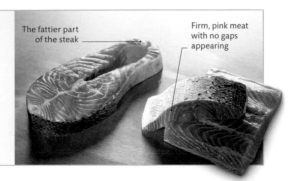

The fattier part of the steak

Firm, pink meat with no gaps appearing

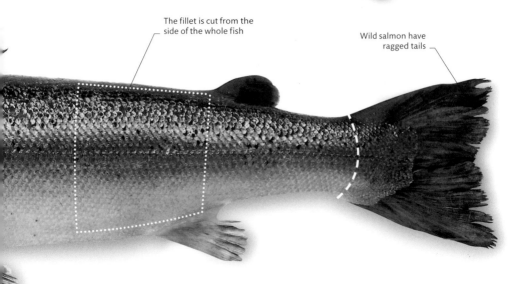

The fillet is cut from the side of the whole fish

Wild salmon have ragged tails

AVAILABILITY

Wild Pacific salmon is in season between June and September. There are five main species: chinook and coho varieties are held to have the best flavour, but are not usually sold raw outside North America; keta (or chum) and sockeye varieties can be found fresh in other parts of the world; pink salmon is usually sold frozen or canned. Farmed Atlantic salmon is available all year round globally.

SUSTAINABILITY

Responsibly managed wild Pacific salmon from the North-east Pacific is best. Wild Atlantic salmon is vastly depleted; most are now farmed, which can have environmental issues. Look for organic farmed fish or those from closed tanks (not open nets).

JOHN DORY
matō dai

This fish has a distinctive spot behind its gills, which gives it its other name – St. Peter's fish. The spot is said to denote the place where St. Peter put his thumb when picking it up. John Dory are rarely found in Japanese waters so are less common on Japanese sushi bar menus, but their firm, delicate-tasting white meat makes them suitable for any type of sushi and a very popular sushi ingredient in Australia.

John Dory fillets

John Dory has a heavy bone, which makes it easier to fillet; it is not very fleshy.

Relatively small and expensive fillets

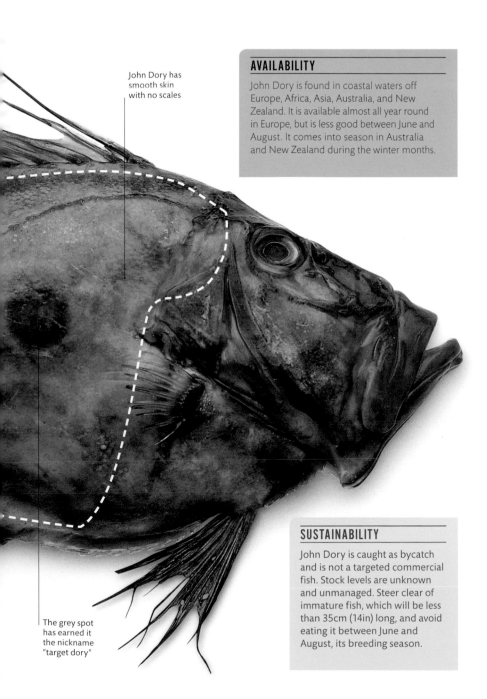

John Dory has smooth skin with no scales

John Dory is found in coastal waters off Europe, Africa, Asia, Australia, and New Zealand. It is available almost all year round in Europe, but is less good between June and August. It comes into season in Australia and New Zealand during the winter months.

SUSTAINABILITY

John Dory is caught as bycatch and is not a targeted commercial fish. Stock levels are unknown and unmanaged. Steer clear of immature fish, which will be less than 35cm (14in) long, and avoid eating it between June and August, its breeding season.

The grey spot has earned it the nickname "target dory"

SEA BASS

suzuki

The Japanese regard the white flesh of the sea bass nearly as highly as they do tai (red snapper) and associate the fish with success in life – another name for it is shusse uo, meaning "advancement in life" or "promotion" fish. This is because, as it grows, the sea bass develops through a series of stages, starting off in fresh water and ending up in the sea. It is known by a different name at each stage and only when the sea bass has lived in the sea and grown to a particular size does it earn the name suzuki. The fish has firm white meat with a delicate flavour and is a good topping for hand-formed sushi. Cut paper thin, it makes elegant sashimi.

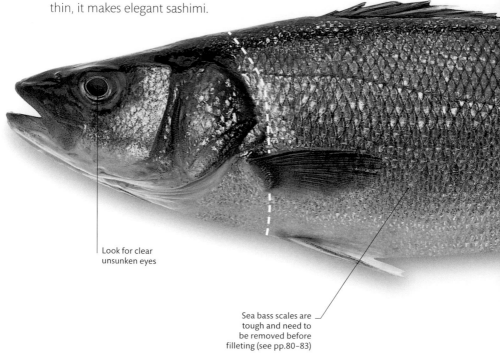

Look for clear
unsunken eyes

Sea bass scales are
tough and need to
be removed before
filleting (see pp.80–83)

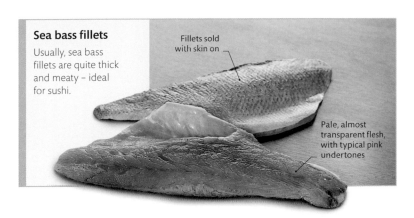

Sea bass fillets

Usually, sea bass fillets are quite thick and meaty – ideal for sushi.

Fillets sold with skin on

Pale, almost transparent flesh, with typical pink undertones

Spines and fins are usually intact on wild sea bass

AVAILABILITY

There are various types of sea bass found all over the world. Wild sea bass are in season in early summer in Japan, all year round in North America, late summer in Australia, and winter in Europe. Farmed sea bass are widely available and reasonably priced. Sea bass should not be confused with the Patagonian toothfish, a vulnerable species, often sold as Chilean sea bass.

SUSTAINABILITY

Avoid wild European sea bass, which are in decline – those farmed organically or in closed tanks are more sustainable. Choose Atlantic and Pacific sea bass caught using handlines or traps to reduce habitat impact; avoid those caught with trawls.

RED SNAPPER
tai

The Japanese consider *tai* to be the best and most noble fish in the sea and the "true" *tai* (*ma dai*), from the Seto Inland Sea, to be the finest of all. Its firm pink-and-white, broad-flaked flesh is delicately flavoured. A whole, handsome grilled *tai* with its tail pointing up on the New Year's Day celebration table is as important as a roast turkey at Thanksgiving or Christmas in the West. Its demand far exceeds its supply, so it's no wonder that the name *tai* has been added to many non-related species. Real *tai* is only available in Japan, but red snapper, sea bream, and porgy, which are often translated as *tai*, are close substitutes.

AVAILABILITY

Ma dai are at their best in spring in Japan, while the North American substitute, porgy, come into season during September and May. In Europe, red snapper and sea bream are available between June and December; in Australia and New Zealand, pink snapper, also known as Australasian snapper or just plain "snapper", are most plentiful in the autumn and winter months.

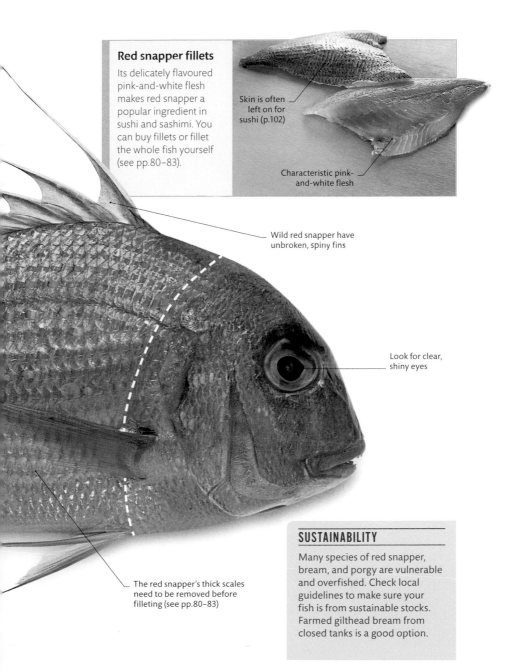

Red snapper fillets

Its delicately flavoured pink-and-white flesh makes red snapper a popular ingredient in sushi and sashimi. You can buy fillets or fillet the whole fish yourself (see pp.80–83).

Skin is often left on for sushi (p.102)

Characteristic pink-and-white flesh

Wild red snapper have unbroken, spiny fins

Look for clear, shiny eyes

The red snapper's thick scales need to be removed before filleting (see pp.80–83)

SUSTAINABILITY

Many species of red snapper, bream, and porgy are vulnerable and overfished. Check local guidelines to make sure your fish is from sustainable stocks. Farmed gilthead bream from closed tanks is a good option.

FILLETING ROUND FISH
for sushi and sashimi

It is more economical to buy a whole fish; it's also easier to assess its freshness. The Japanese call this method of filleting *sanmai oroshi*, or "three-piece filleting", as the end result is two fillets and the skeleton. Use a sharp knife, and work within easy access of running water.

PREPARATION TIME about 15 minutes

EQUIPMENT

fish scaler | large plastic bag | pair of small tweezers or pliers

METHOD

1 Scale the fish by holding the head and firmly drawing the scaler from the tail to the head. Hold the fish under cold running water or place inside a large plastic bag to catch the flying fish scales.

2 Insert the tip of a sharp knife into the belly and cut open the underside of the fish from the gills to the fin near the tail. Take care not to damage any internal organs.

3 Cut from the tail fin to the tail. Open up the slit and remove the innards by pulling them firmly towards the tail. Discard the innards, then wash and clean the cavity and the knife.

4 With the head facing you, carefully insert the knife into the back of the fish at the tail. Cut along towards the head with the knife blade resting on the backbone.

5 Hold the fish by its gills on one side and cut through the body to the spine. Turn the fish over and cut through the other side. Finally, cut through the spine to remove the head.

CONTINUED ▶

6 At the tail, insert the knife through the slit made on its back to the slit made in its underside so that the blade passes just over the skeleton. Keeping the blade flat and working away from the tail, cut the fillet loose with a firm sawing action. Use the ribs and backbone to guide the blade. Slice through the skin that attaches the fillet at the tail.

7 Turn the fish over and repeat steps 4 and 6, then cut away the second fillet.

8 You should have 2 large equal-sized and -shaped fillets and the skeleton.

9 With the knife almost horizontal, carefully cut the stomach cavity lining and any rib bones away. Run your hands lightly over the surface of the fillets to feel for any pin bones and remove with tweezers or small pliers. Trim the edges of the fillets.

10 To skin the fillets, rub some salt on your fingers to provide a better grip. Grasp the tail and cut at a shallow angle as far as the skin, taking care not to cut through it.

11 Keeping the blade still and almost parallel with the chopping board, pull carefully on the fish skin, working it from side to side so that the skin comes away from the fillet.

TURBOT

hirame

There is no direct translation for turbot, but the Japanese classify all flatfish with both eyes on the left of the head as *hirame*. Similar-looking but smaller fish from the Indian Ocean, the South China Sea, and off the coast of Queensland, Australia are often exported to Japan as *hirame*. Of all *hirame*, the white flesh of the turbot is considered to have the most exquisite flavour and a meaty, succulent texture. It is excellent eaten raw in sushi and as sashimi.

Fresh fish do not have sunken eyes

Turbot fillets

The outer edges of the fillets are considered to be a delicacy as they are slightly crunchy and each fish yields only small strips.

Ask your fishmonger not to remove the edges

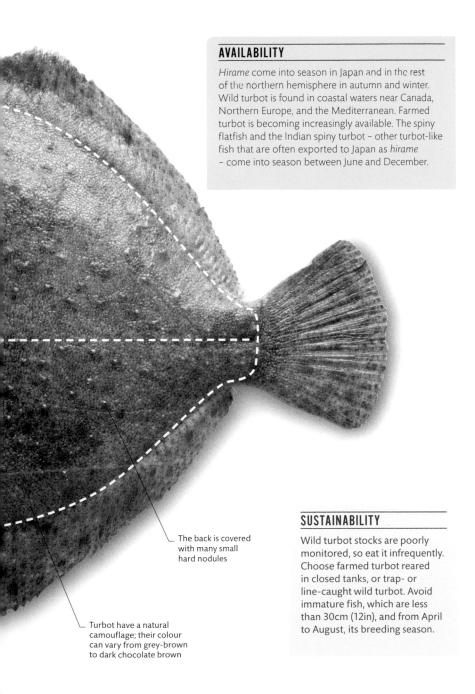

Hirame come into season in Japan and in the rest of the northern hemisphere in autumn and winter. Wild turbot is found in coastal waters near Canada, Northern Europe, and the Mediterranean. Farmed turbot is becoming increasingly available. The spiny flatfish and the Indian spiny turbot – other turbot-like fish that are often exported to Japan as *hirame* – come into season between June and December.

The back is covered with many small hard nodules

Turbot have a natural camouflage; their colour can vary from grey-brown to dark chocolate brown

SUSTAINABILITY

Wild turbot stocks are poorly monitored, so eat it infrequently. Choose farmed turbot reared in closed tanks, or trap- or line-caught wild turbot. Avoid immature fish, which are less than 30cm (12in), and from April to August, its breeding season.

BRILL
hirame

Brill is a left-eyed flatfish (which the Japanese classify as *hirame*) and belongs to the turbot family. Slightly smaller and with sweet, firm flesh, brill is often used as an alternative to turbot and is a popular ingredient in sushi. It can camouflage itself by changing the colour of the skin on its back to match the seabed where it lives.

A fresh brill has a full, plump head

Each side of the fish produces two fillets (see pp.92–95)

AVAILABILITY

Found in the Eastern Atlantic, Mediterranean, and Black Sea, brill is available in Europe for most of the year but is at its best in autumn and winter. There are other types of left-eyed flatfish available around the world that are similar to brill and can be used for sushi in the same way. However, avoid megrim, which is similar in appearance but has a slightly watery, bland flavour that is not good in sushi.

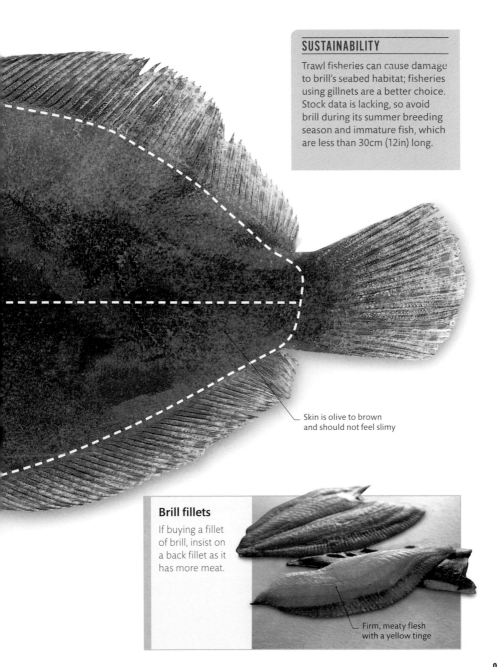

SUSTAINABILITY

Trawl fisheries can cause damage to brill's seabed habitat; fisheries using gillnets are a better choice. Stock data is lacking, so avoid brill during its summer breeding season and immature fish, which are less than 30cm (12in) long.

Skin is olive to brown and should not feel slimy

Brill fillets

If buying a fillet of brill, insist on a back fillet as it has more meat.

Firm, meaty flesh with a yellow tinge

LEMON SOLE

karei

Despite its name, lemon sole is no relation of Dover sole and is in fact a type of flounder. The Japanese regard it as one of the *karei* family: flatfish with both eyes on the right side of the head. Among the *karei* group, lemon sole is often overshadowed by the other more highly prized flatfish such as halibut, flounder, and plaice. However, its succulent white flesh makes it suitable for all types of sushi and sashimi.

Lemon sole fillets

With a delicate, almost sweet, flavour and succulent texture, lemon sole is a popular sushi ingredient outside Japan.

Thicker back fillets are better for sushi and sashimi

AVAILABILITY

Lemon sole is found in the seas of northern Europe: the North Atlantic, the North Sea, and the Norwegian Sea. They are caught throughout the year, but are at their best between September and March. There are various types of flounder available throughout the year in North America, but should be avoided from April to September as this is when they breed and the flesh tends to be less flavoursome.

Look for clean, shiny, and moist skin

If the fish has a fat belly, it may be pregnant

SUSTAINABILITY

Choose net-caught lemon sole over those caught by trawl. Avoid immature fish (less than 25cm/ 10in) and its breeding season from April to August. Pacific flounder is generally more sustainable than Atlantic species. Check for local certified fisheries.

HALIBUT
ohyō garei

A member of the *karei* family (flatfish with both eyes on the right side of the head), halibut is the largest of the flatfish. It can reach more than 4m (13ft) in length and more than 300kg (660lb) in weight. As it is a slow-growing fish, taking 7–11 years to mature and living for up to 50 years, it is very vulnerable to overfishing and has become scarce in the North Atlantic. Its lean, firm, white flesh and mild, sweet flavour makes it a popular ingredient for sushi and sashimi, but choose sustainable sources carefully.

Halibut steak

Because of the size of the fish, halibut is often sold in steak form outside of Japan.

Bone is removed before being sliced for sushi (see pp.98–99)

AVAILABILITY

Atlantic halibut is native to the North Atlantic ocean, from Canada to Norway, but it is endangered in the wild. Farmed Atlantic halibut is increasingly available in Europe and North America. Wild Pacific halibut is found in the North Pacific ocean and is at its best between April and September.

SUSTAINABILITY

Wild Atlantic halibut is an endangered species, so avoid it. Choose farmed Atlantic halibut from closed tanks instead. Wild Pacific halibut is a better option, as the fisheries are well managed.

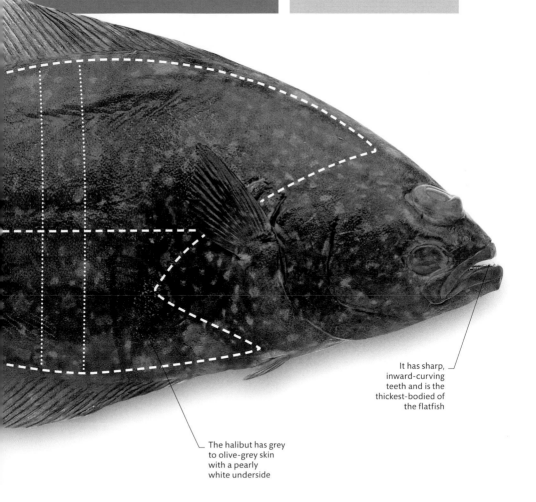

It has sharp, inward-curving teeth and is the thickest-bodied of the flatfish

The halibut has grey to olive-grey skin with a pearly white underside

FILLETING FLATFISH
for sushi and sashimi

Japanese sushi chefs traditionally fillet flatfish using the *gomai oroshi* or "five-piece filleting" method, so called because the end result is four fillets and the skeleton. Most flatfish have scales that are invisible to the naked eye; these must be removed by skinning for sushi and sashimi.

PREPARATION TIME about 15 minutes

EQUIPMENT
pair of small tweezers or pliers

METHOD

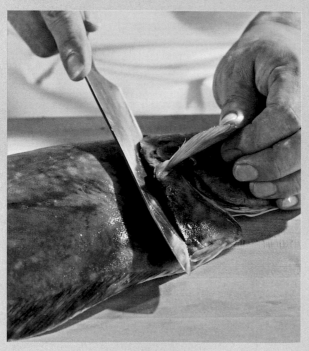

1 Insert the blade at a 45° angle just behind the central fin and cut off the head. The innards should come away as you pull off the head.

Work on a meticulously clean surface

2 Place the fish on its lighter-coloured belly and cut around one side of the fish just inside the outer fin.

3 Turn the fish round and cut around the other side.

4 Starting at the tail, cut into the fish as far as the backbone. Cut down the middle of the fish, working towards the front of it.

CONTINUED ▶

5 Turn the fish around so the tail is facing you. With the knife at a slight angle, ease the blade into the central cut, feeling for when it reaches the bones. Using the bones to guide the knife, work down the length of the fish, cutting the fillet away from the skeleton. Long, smooth strokes will give a cleaner, less jagged cut.

6 Turn the fish around and do the same to the fillet on the other side of the fish, this time starting at the tail end.

7 Flatfish are nearly symmetrical, so simply turn the fish over and repeat steps 4 to 6 to cut the fillets from the other side of the fish.

8 Cutting at an angle, carefully remove the stomach cavity lining and pull out any little bones with small tweezers or pliers. Trim the fillets to an even shape.

9 You should have 4 fillets. To skin them, see p.83, steps 10 and 11. After skinning, you can slice them as needed for sushi and sashimi (see pp.96–97).

SLICING FISH FILLETS
for sushi and sashimi

Although it is ideal to buy a whole fish, it is not always practical. Large fish such as tuna, salmon, or halibut are usually sold in blocks or fillets. This technique shows how to slice fish fillets to use in different types of sushi and sashimi. Start with a skinless fish fillet, weighing about 300g (10oz) and 2.5–5cm (1–2in) thick.

PREPARATION TIME 15 minutes

METHOD

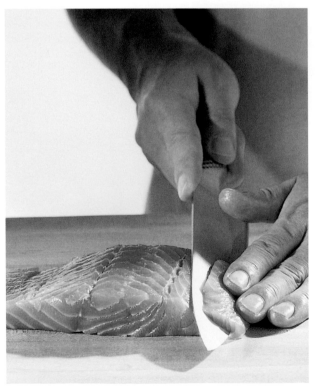

1 For hand-formed sushi (see pp.222–39), cut diagonal slices about 5mm (¼in) thick. Hold the knife at a 45° angle to the fish. Resting your fingertips lightly on the fish, gently work the knife through the fish to produce even slices. The first slice may not be suitable for hand-formed sushi, but it can be used for thin roll sushi.

3 For pressed sushi (see pp.180–93) and wafer-thin sashimi (see p.248–49), cut large, flat pieces of fish. Resting one hand lightly on the fillet and keeping the blade parallel to it, carefully cut as thin a slice as you can – about 3mm (⅛in) thick – from the top of the fillet. Repeat as needed for more slices.

2 For hand-rolled sushi and thick roll sushi (see pp.216–19 and pp.200–03), slice the fillet as for hand-formed sushi (see step 1), but cut the pieces slightly thicker. Next, slice the pieces lengthways into 1cm (½in) square sticks. For hand-rolled sushi, each stick should be about 6cm (2½in) long to fit the cone shapes.

4 For scattered sushi (see pp.136–59) or sashimi (see pp.240–45), cut slices 1cm (½in) thick. The slices can also be cut into strips for rolled sushi.

SLICING FISH STEAKS
for sushi and sashimi

Many large fish are often sold as steaks and need some preparation before they can be sliced for sushi. Once the bones and skin have been removed and the fish shaped into blocks, it can be sliced for scattered, rolled, and hand-formed sushi and sashimi. Use a fish steak weighing about 250g (9oz).

PREPARATION TIME 15 minutes

EQUIPMENT
pair of small tweezers or pliers

METHOD

1 Place the steak on the chopping board skin-side down. Hold it securely in position and cut the steak in half, working a sharp knife carefully under the central bone.

2 Position the half of the steak with the bone skin-side down. Holding it steady, repeat step 1 and carefully cut out the bone.

3 Remove any bones that might still be in the flesh (see p.101, step 5) and, using a sharp knife, trim any fatty tissue from the fillet.

4 Position the fish skin-side down. Holding the blade parallel to the chopping board, carefully cut off the skin.

5 Cut the resulting evenly shaped pieces of fish into 1cm (½in) strips for scattered sushi, hand-formed sushi, or sashimi.

6 Alternatively, cut the slices in half lengthways into strips of about pencil thickness, and use for rolled sushi.

MARINATING MACKEREL
shime saba

Mackerel is an excellent fish: plentiful, available all year round, inexpensive, and very healthy. However, it spoils quickly so it is rarely eaten raw, even in Japan. Marinating mackerel in salt and vinegar makes it last longer, but also enhances its flavour and firms the flesh to make it easier to slice. You can prepare it in advance – once marinated, wrap in cling film and keep in the refrigerator for up to 3 days.

PREPARATION TIME 2–3 hours

EQUIPMENT

bamboo strainer or colander | pair of kitchen tweezers or pliers

INGREDIENTS

per 150g (5oz) mackerel fillet

about 2 tbsp sea salt

125ml (4fl oz) rice vinegar

½ tbsp mirin or ¾ tbsp caster sugar

½ tsp salt

Salt draws moisture from the fish to help preserve it

METHOD

1 Place the mackerel fillets in a large bowl, and pour over the sea salt. Gently rub the mackerel fillets with the sea salt, ensuring they are evenly covered.

2 Place the fillets on a Japanese-style bamboo strainer or in a colander. Leave for at least 30 minutes, preferably 1 hour, to allow juices drawn out by the salt to drain off. Rinse under cold running water and pat dry with kitchen paper.

3 Mix together the vinegar, mirin or sugar, and salt in a plastic or glass container large enough to hold the fillets in one layer. Add the mackerel to the bowl and set aside to marinate for 1–2 hours.

4 Take the fillets out of the vinegar mixture, and pat dry with kitchen paper. The flesh should have whitened. Slowly peel off the papery thin outer skin, starting at the head. Don't worry if some of the iridescent underskin also comes off.

5 Place the fillets on a chopping board and run the tips of your fingers lightly up and down them to feel for any small bones. Use tweezers to remove any that you find, and a sharp knife to trim and shape the fillets, if necessary.

TENERIZING FISH SKIN
for sushi and sashimi

Fish in sushi and sashimi are usually served skinless, but some medium-sized fish, especially red snapper and silver bream, have deliciously chewy, faintly sweet-tasting skin, which the Japanese feel a shame to waste. This technique of tenderizing fish skin by brief blanching is called matsukawa-zukuri, or "pine bark method", as it slightly shrinks the skin and makes it resemble the bark of pine trees. Use any size of fish fillet, but it must be scaled first (see p.80, Step 1).

PREPARATION TIME 10 minutes

EQUIPMENT
bamboo strainer or colander | fukin (Japanese cloth) or tea towel

---

METHOD

1 Place the scaled fillet skin-side up on a Japanese-style bamboo strainer set over a shallow dish, or in a colander in the sink. Cover with a clean fukin or tea towel.

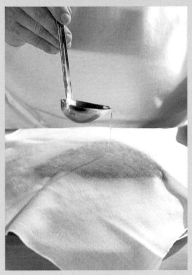

2 Bring 300ml (10fl oz) water to the boil. Carefully pour the freshly boiled water over the covered fillet.

3 Cool the fillet by plunging it into cold water or by holding it under a cold-running tap for a few minutes. The flesh should have whitened and the skin shrunk.

4 For scattered sushi or sashimi, slice the fillet into strips about 1cm (½in) thick.

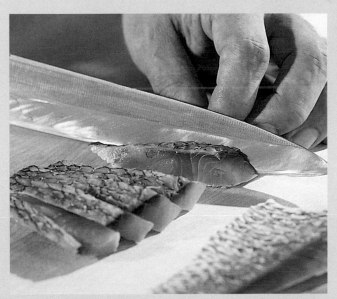

SHELLFISH AND ROE
kai rui

As an island nation surrounded by seas, Japan features all manner of seafood in its cuisine, including shellfish and roe in sushi and sashimi. It is vital that you buy the **freshest** possible **shellfish.** Check the following to ensure freshness:

• Scallops and oysters are **bought alive**. They should not float in water and should feel heavy; their shells should remain tightly closed and not be chipped.

• Select prawns with **clear, undamaged shells**.

• If buying a whole octopus, check that the **eyes are clear** and bright, not cloudy or sunken.

• Sea urchin is almost always bought ready-prepared, removed from its spiky shell. It should be a **bright** mustard colour and **moist** but not wet. Avoid ones with a strong smell of ammonia.

• Fish roes tend to have **longer shelf-lives** as they are often sold in jars or tins, which makes them good store-cupboard ingredients for sushi.

CRAB
kani

Whatever the local variety may be, in a sushi shop, crab is always served cooked and referred to as *kani*. The "California roll", an invention originally created for American palates, uses cooked crabmeat, avocado, and mayonnaise in an inside-out roll sushi. If the thought of buying a live crab and boiling it whole is too daunting, buy a ready-boiled or, better still, a dressed crab for making sushi at home.

Cooked crab

It takes some effort to extract the meat from a cooked crab (see pp.108–11). Only white crabmeat is used for sushi.

White, coral-flecked crabmeat

AVAILABILITY

Crab is available all over the world, but local varieties are often best for freshness and flavour. Different crabs have different spawning seasons, so some may be best in the summer while others are best in the winter – ask your fishmonger what's in season. Frozen white crabmeat can be used for sushi, but beware of "crab sticks", which are often made with cheap, processed fish, not crab.

SUSTAINABILITY

Make sure the crab you buy is the minimum landing size for its species – smaller ones will be immature. Avoid egg-bearing females as well. Pots or traps are the most sustainable catch methods as they reduce habitat damage and bycatch.

Crab claws contain sweet, white meat and are bigger on male crabs

Male crabmeat is not as sweet as that of a female. A male crab has a small flap, or "apron", under its body, which is big on a female

PREPARING CRAB

for sushi

Cooking a live crab at home isn't for the faint hearted, and if it isn't done expertly and humanely it can cause unnecessary suffering for the animal and produce disappointing results. For these reasons, I would recommend buying crabs that are ready-cooked or ready-dressed. Only the white meat is used for making sushi, not the more strongly flavoured brown meat.

PREPARATION TIME 15–20 minutes

EQUIPMENT

claw cracker or nutcracker | seafood pick or flat metal skewer

METHOD

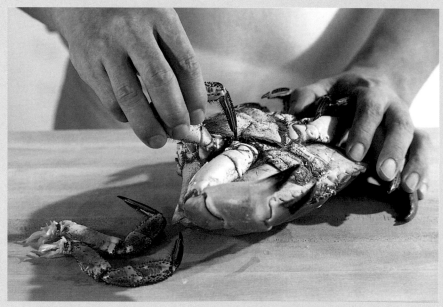

1 Set the cooked crab on its back on a chopping board, and twist and break the claws and legs from the body.

2 Use a claw cracker or nutcracker to crack open the large claws. All the crab's legs will contain some meat, although the very small legs will hardly be worth the effort.

3 Flake the meat from the cracked claws using a seafood pick or a flat metal skewer.

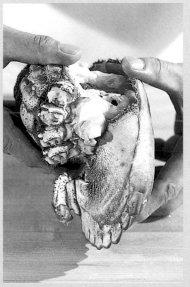

4 Using the heel of a large, sharp knife, firmly cut through the join where the crab's tail meets the body.

5 Ease the main part of the crab's body out of the shell.

CONTINUED ▶

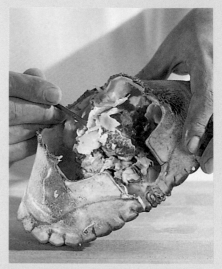

6 Most of the white meat is contained in the body of the crab, while the brown meat is left in the shell.

7 The brown meat and red coral can easily be scraped from the shell if desired. Be sure to discard the pale paper-like head sac and stomach found just behind the crab's mouth.

8 Remove and discard the grey-looking gills or "dead man's fingers" from the sides of the central body section.

9 Pull the tail flap or apron from the main body section of the crab.

10 Using a heavy knife, cut the body in half to get to the meat.

11 Clean away any remaining coral or brown meat using a seafood pick or skewer.

12 Carefully pick the white meat out of all the sections of body, discarding any small pieces of membrane or shell.

13 If necessary, cut the body into quarters to enable you to reach all the inaccessible areas and remove the white meat.

LOBSTER
ise ebi

Revered as the king of the prawn family with its hard armour and firm, succulent flesh, lobster commands high prices. There are two main types of lobster – "true" lobsters are those with large claws; those without large claws are known as spiny lobsters. The latter type is an essential item for celebratory feasts in Japan. Both types of lobster can vary in length from 30–100cm (12–40in) and weigh as much as 3–4kg (6–9lb). Buy small to medium-sized lobsters as larger ones tend to have drier, less succulent flesh and a blander flavour. Large lobsters are also usually female, and therefore important breeding stock for wild lobster populations.

Turn the lobster over and check that the tail is filled with meat

The muscular tail contains the densest and sweetest meat for sushi

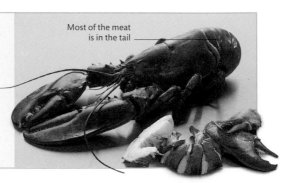

Cooked lobster

Lobsters come in a wide variety of colours but they all turn a deep burgundy red when properly cooked.

Most of the meat is in the tail

Choose lobsters with the fewest barnacles

Claws should feel heavy and solid

AVAILABILITY

The east coast of North America is the major source of true lobster; the high season is between June and October. In Europe, true lobster is available all year round, although they are best between October and June. Australia is the main provider of spiny lobster, where it is in season from mid-November to May. The west coast of North America is also a good source of spiny lobster.

SUSTAINABILITY

True lobster is slow-growing and both American and European stocks are decreasing. American lobster is also associated with bycatch of endangered species. Buy from certified fisheries only, or try spiny lobster from the US west coast or Australia instead.

PREPARING LOBSTER
for sushi

Cooking live lobsters, like cooking live crabs, is better left to experts who can perform the procedure humanely and efficiently. I would recommend buying a ready-cooked lobster, which is available from most fishmongers. The following technique demonstrates how to extract the meat from a cooked lobster; only the white meat is used for sushi.

PREPARATION TIME 10–15 minutes

EQUIPMENT

heavy knife or nutcracker | seafood pick or flat metal skewer

---

METHOD

1 Most of the white meat is found in the muscular tail and, for clawed lobsters, in the two large claws.

2 Use the heel of a heavy knife blade to crack open the claws, or alternatively, use a nutcracker. Pick out the meat with a seafood pick or flat metal skewer.

4 Using a sharp, heavy knife, cut through the translucent shell covering the bottom of the tail on both sides, at the point where it meets the upper shell.

3 Grasp the lobster in both hands and detach the head where it joins the body.

5 Pull away and discard the translucent covering to get to the meat.

6 Pull the white meat out of the tail section – it should come out of the shell in one large piece.

PRAWNS
ebi

There are many varieties and sizes of prawn: large warm-water prawns and small, sweet cold-water prawns (sometimes called shrimp), and saltwater or freshwater types. For sushi, they are all referred to as *ebi*. They are usually served cooked and have a delicate flavour and a firm texture. Raw cold-water prawn, *ama ebi*, is considered a great delicacy among sushi connoisseurs. It has a jewel-like, glossy, almost transparent appearance and is sweet in flavour with a tender texture. Demand for prawns is more than wild supplies can meet, so even sushi bars in Japan import frozen stocks. Many prawns are farmed.

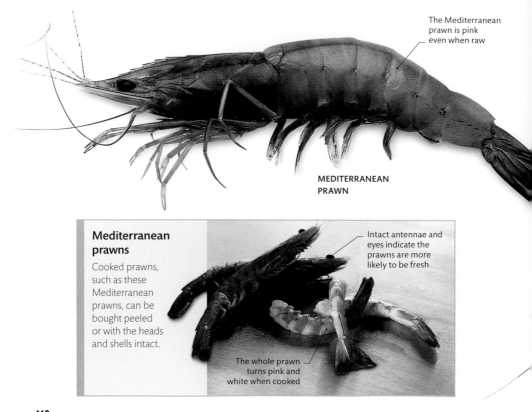

The Mediterranean prawn is pink even when raw

MEDITERRANEAN PRAWN

Mediterranean prawns

Cooked prawns, such as these Mediterranean prawns, can be bought peeled or with the heads and shells intact.

Intact antennae and eyes indicate the prawns are more likely to be fresh

The whole prawn turns pink and white when cooked

AVAILABILITY

In general, prawns that live in warmer waters are larger than those that live in cold oceans. Most warm-water prawns are farmed; they are available globally all year round. Australia's wild warm-water prawns are in season from April until December. Cold-water prawns are caught in the North Atlantic, North Pacific, and Arctic oceans, especially in winter. They are often sold cooked. The raw prawn, *ama ebi*, is best bought ready-prepared from specialist Japanese shops.

SUSTAINABILITY

Farmed warm-water prawns can be a good choice if they come from organic or certified sources where environmetal standards are high. For cold-water prawns, the most sustainable fisheries use sorting grids to reduce bycatch. Look for certified fisheries as the best choice.

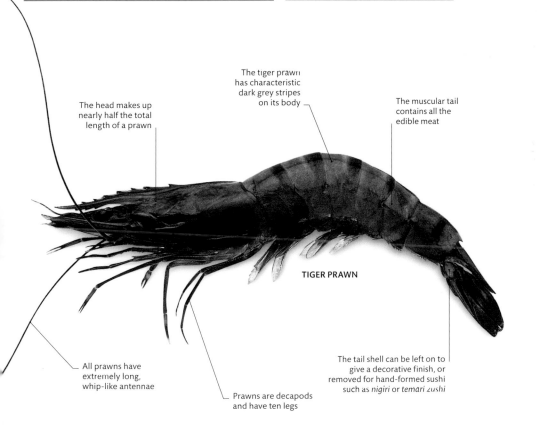

The tiger prawn has characteristic dark grey stripes on its body

The head makes up nearly half the total length of a prawn

The muscular tail contains all the edible meat

All prawns have extremely long, whip-like antennae

TIGER PRAWN

Prawns are decapods and have ten legs

The tail shell can be left on to give a decorative finish, or removed for hand-formed sushi such as *nigiri* or *temari zushi*

117

PREPARING PRAWNS
for sushi

Their firm, sweet flesh makes king and tiger prawns popular ingredients in all types of sushi. Inserting a skewer along the underside of the prawn before cooking prevents it from curling. Take care not to overcook them as this can give them a rubbery texture.

PREPARATION TIME 10 minutes

EQUIPMENT
bamboo skewers

METHOD

1 Holding each prawn with the legs facing upwards, insert a wooden skewer under the transparent shell, where the head joins the tail. Take care not to pierce the flesh. Place in a large pan of boiling water, and cook until the flesh turns white and pink, about 2–3 minutes. Drain and set aside to cool.

2 Remove the skewer from the prawn. Gently but firmly, pull the head to separate it from the body. Discard the head.

3 Holding the prawn with the legs facing upwards, use your thumbs to remove the legs and peel away the outer shell. Leave the tail intact.

4 Using a sharp knife, cut along the underside of the prawn until you reach the dark vein that runs the length of its body.

5 Use a knife or the wooden skewer to scrape out the dark vein. You may need to wipe any remaining vein away with a damp cloth. You now have a butterflied, flattened-out prawn.

6 Trim and tidy the ends of the tail. This gives an elegant presentation but for some sushi, such as hand-formed sushi, you might want to carefully pull off the tail shell.

SQUID AND OCTOPUS
ika / tako

The Japanese word *ika* refers to many different varieties of squid, but *ma ika* and *yari ika* are most preferred for sushi. Always buy squid fresh, if possible; it freezes well if you have too much, which makes it a convenient ingredient for home sushi-making. The octopus feeds on other fish and shellfish such as crab, lobster, and scallops – this gourmet diet makes it high in protein and gives it excellent flavour. It has a firm texture and makes a very good sushi topping. Larger octopus have thicker tentacles which are easier to slice for hand-formed sushi (pp.124–25).

Fresh octopus should look shiny and firm and smell like the ocean, never fishy

OCTOPUS

Cooked octopus

For both sushi and sashimi, only cooked tentacles are used.

Deep red-purple colour when cooked

SQUID

Squid is nearly always served raw. Its pearly white, glossy flesh has a sticky, almost resistant, texture

The body and tentacles are used to make many different types of sushi

Only the octopus's tentacles are used as a sushi topping

AVAILABILITY

Squid and octopus are available all year, but squid is at its best in Europe in autumn and winter, and during spring in North America; octopus is at its best in winter and spring in the northern hemisphere. Look for squid and octopus that still have their tentacles intact and most of their skin on – these are signs of good handling. Remember, high quality frozen squid or octopus is a lot better than low quality fresh.

SUSTAINABILITY

Both squid and octopus are fairly resilient but check current guidelines as some stocks are under pressure. Fishing methods cause concern over bycatch and habitat damage – avoid fisheries in the Indo-Pacific region and those that use trawls especially.

PREPARING SQUID
for sushi

A popular sushi ingredient, squid is extremely simple to clean. Choose only the freshest squid – it should look glossy and have shiny black eyes. Use the method below to prepare squid for scattered sushi (pp.136–59) or hand-formed sushi (pp.222–39). For Stuffed Squid Sushi (pp.164–67), keep the body and tentacles intact.

PREPARATION TIME 10 minutes

EQUIPMENT
clean cloth or tea towel

METHOD

1 Detach the head and tentacles by firmly pulling them from the body. Cut the tentacles off and keep, if required, but discard the head and innards.

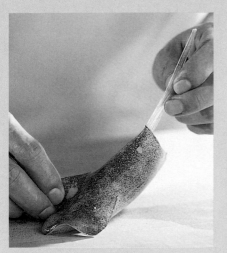

2 Pull the translucent, quill-shaped piece of cartilage out of the body and discard it.

3 If stuffing the squid, keep the body whole and go to the next step. Otherwise, insert a sharp knife into the body and carefully slit it down one side.

4 Either open the body and lay it flat, skin-side up, or lay the intact body on a clean surface or chopping board. Grasp the two triangular fins and pull upwards. Discard the fins and the skin.

5 Use a clean, damp cloth to wipe away the mucous lining on one side and any pieces of skin left behind on the other. If using the squid whole, turn it inside out and wipe with a cloth.

PREPARING OCTOPUS

for sushi

Although the whole of an octopus can be eaten raw, normally only the boiled tentacles are used for sushi. Boiling tenderizes the meat and gives it a sweet flavour, but keep the heat as low as possible as rapid boiling toughens it. Fresh octopus needs to be rubbed clean with salt before cooking. Clean the suckers and ends of tentacles as they may contain mud or sand.

PREPARATION TIME 45 minutes

INGREDIENTS AND EQUIPMENT

200g (7oz) salt, or enough to coat the tentacles | bamboo strainer or colander

METHOD

1 Using a sharp knife, cut the tentacles off just below the eyes.

2 Put the tentacles in a bowl or on a chopping board and pour over the salt. Rub the salt into the tentacles to tenderize and clean them.

3 Bring a large pan of salted water to the boil and add the tentacles. Bring back to the boil, then reduce the heat and simmer gently for about 10 minutes.

4 Drain in a Japanese-style bamboo strainer or colander, and set aside to cool. The skin should have turned a deep pink/red with the tentacles tightly curled, showing clean white suckers.

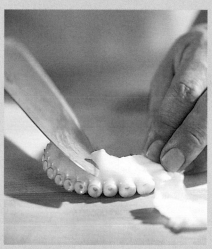

5 Cut the tentacles away from the central section which contains the octopus's mouth parts or "beak". This section should be discarded.

6 With the blade of the knife at a 45° angle to the chopping board, cut the tentacles diagonally into 3–4mm (⅛in) slices.

OYSTERS AND SCALLOPS
kaki / hotate gai

Shellfish such as oysters and scallops have been harvested and eaten by humans since prehistoric times, and there are many varieties found all over the world. With their light, salty flavour, raw oysters are usually served as a topping for battleship sushi (pp.232–35). The delicately flavoured, soft flesh of the scallop is served as a topping for hand-formed sushi (pp.224–31) and sashimi. The scallop's orange roe is not used for sushi.

Oyster shells are often dotted with barnacles

OYSTERS

Fresh oysters should always be firmly closed

All of the watery grey body of the oyster is edible

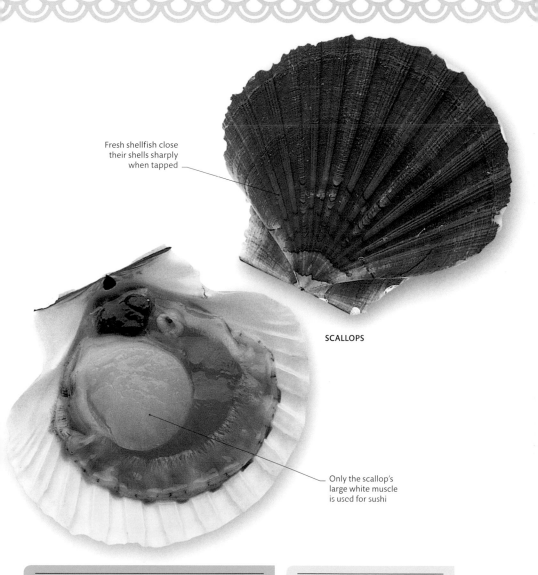

Fresh shellfish close
their shells sharply
when tapped

SCALLOPS

Only the scallop's
large white muscle
is used for sushi

AVAILABILITY

Farmed oysters are available all year round in most parts of the world, but it is best to avoid them during the breeding season, which is in summer in both the northern and southern hemispheres. Pacific oysters are a commonly farmed variety. Both wild and farmed scallops are available worldwide, but they are tastier in the winter months.

SUSTAINABILITY

Farmed oysters and scallops are a sustainable choice, as shellfish cultivation has a low impact on the environment. Wild oyster and scallop stocks are vulnerable in some areas, so check local guidelines before you buy.

PREPARING OYSTERS AND SCALLOPS
for sushi

Because of their runny consistency, oysters are used in battleship rolls (see pp.232–35). Thin slices of raw scallop, which have a delicate sweet flavour, are used as a topping for hand-formed sushi (see pp.222–39) and for scattered sushi (see pp.136–59). Discard oysters and scallops with cracked, chipped, or broken shells.

PREPARATION TIME about 1 minute per oyster or scallop

EQUIPMENT

oyster knife or any thin, sharp knife | tea towel

SHUCKING OYSTERS

1 Place the oyster on a firm surface. Use a tea towel to protect your hand from the sharp shell. Work the knife into the hinge – the narrowest point of the shell. Twist the blade to separate the shells slightly. Slide the blade into the oyster shell, keeping it flat against the upper shell, and scrape it from one side to the other to cut the muscle. You should be able to remove the upper shell easily now.

2 Cut through the muscle that attaches the oyster to the lower shell and carefully remove the oyster. Use immediately.

SHELLING SCALLOPS

1 Slide an oyster knife or a thin sharp knife into the shell and cut the muscle that attaches the upper and lower shells. Keep the blade flat against the upper shell and work the blade from side to side.

2 Noting the position of the cut part of the muscle, insert the blade under the scallop at the same spot and cut through the muscle attaching the scallop to the lower shell.

3 Tear off the frilly fringe and bright orange coral – only the round, white muscle is used for sushi.

4 Rinse in cold water and cut into thin slices about 3–4mm (⅛in) thick by cutting across the top of the scallop. Use immediately.

FISH ROE, CAVIAR, AND SEA URCHIN

Because of their slippery nature, fish roe, caviar, and sea urchin are usually served in the form of battleship-shaped sushi, where a sheet of nori holds the topping in place. Some of the smaller roes, such as flying fish roe, or *tobiko*, are used as coatings to add colour to inside-out sushi rolls. Fish roe and caviar are considered to be delicacies and often command exorbitant prices. Herring roe, or *kazunoko*, for example, was once so abundant on the coasts of Japan that it was used as fertilizer. These days it is so expensive, it has earned the nickname "yellow diamond".

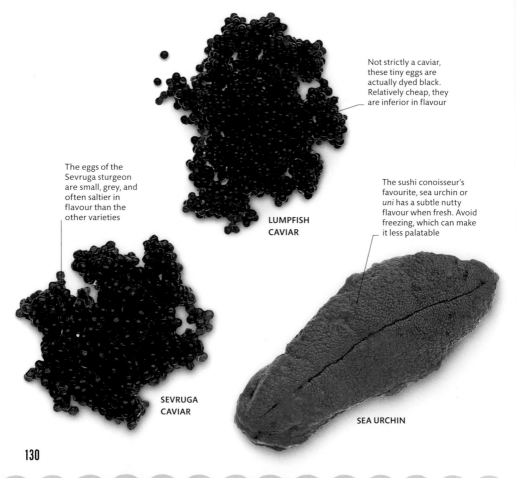

Not strictly a caviar, these tiny eggs are actually dyed black. Relatively cheap, they are inferior in flavour

The eggs of the Sevruga sturgeon are small, grey, and often saltier in flavour than the other varieties

The sushi conoisseur's favourite, sea urchin or *uni* has a subtle nutty flavour when fresh. Avoid freezing, which can make it less palatable

LUMPFISH CAVIAR

SEVRUGA CAVIAR

SEA URCHIN

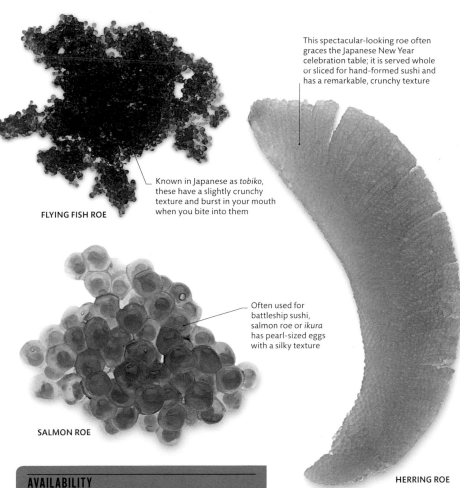

This spectacular-looking roe often graces the Japanese New Year celebration table; it is served whole or sliced for hand-formed sushi and has a remarkable, crunchy texture

Known in Japanese as *tobiko*, these have a slightly crunchy texture and burst in your mouth when you bite into them

FLYING FISH ROE

Often used for battleship sushi, salmon roe or *ikura* has pearl-sized eggs with a silky texture

SALMON ROE

HERRING ROE

AVAILABILITY

Caviar and lumpfish caviar are widely available in small jars or tins. Genuine caviar is expensive and, although not a traditional sushi ingredient, its silky texture and luxurious taste have made it popular amongst more innovative sushi chefs. Once opened, caviar should be refrigerated and used within one week. Salmon roe is available in small jars and can be soaked in sake for 1–2 minutes to separate the eggs. It should also be refrigerated once opened and used within one week. Japan and North America are the primary sources of sea urchin.

SUSTAINABILITY

Look for caviar from responsibly farmed sturgeon, as this is a threatened species in the wild. Look for salmon roe from sustainable salmon (see pp.72–73). Sea urchin stocks are overfished in some areas, so check current guidelines in your country.

131

OTHER SEAFOOD
for sushi

Sushi has a wide variety of toppings and fillings, some familiar and some more unusual than others. You may first come across some of the fish, shellfish, and other seafood listed here in sushi bars, but as you become more confident with sushi-making, consider using some of the following to broaden your range.

King crab legs contain white-and-red meat

ALASKAN KING CRAB
kani

These large crabs are available ready-cooked from most good fishmongers, but tend to be more expensive than other varieties. This is because the wild crabs are caught in autumn to strict quotas and the season is short. King crabs caught in places other than Alaska may be less sustainable options. The legs, which need to be cracked open, contain more of the sweet, white-and-red meat than the body. Alaskan king crab makes a good topping for hand-formed sushi and is often held in place with a strip of nori. Buy fresh crabmeat if possible, but frozen is also available.

CRAYFISH
zarigani

Found in freshwater, crayfish looks like a small lobster, but tastes sweeter. Only the meaty tails are used for sushi; these are usually bought ready-cooked. Most of the crayfish available is farmed, with the biggest producers being the USA and China. American crayfish farmed in the USA is a sustainable choice. However, American crayfish species introduced to other countries, such as the UK, have caused widespread ecological damage. In those cases, choosing locally caught American crayfish helps to control its population.

COMMON CLAM
asari

The small common clam is not usually used in sushi but is often added to soups (see p.54). To clean the grit from clams, put them in a large bowl with a tablespoon of salt, a handful of cornmeal, and enough water to cover them. Refrigerate for 2 hours, then rinse before use. Farmed clams are a sustainable option.

Fresh common clams

ATLANTIC SURF CLAM
uba gai / hokki gai

This large clam is called *uba gai* in Japanese, but is better known as *hokki gai* when used in sushi. It is found in the cold, northern waters of Japan, and in the North Atlantic. It can be eaten either raw or cooked – which makes a very tasty topping for hand-formed sushi. Atlantic surf clam fisheries in North America are regulated by catch quotas.

Cooked Atlantic surf clams

YELLOWTAIL
hamachi

Yellowtail is the common name for a specific type of amberjack native to Japan. It has light golden flesh and very little fat. *Hamachi* is best eaten young when its rich, smooth, buttery texture and slightly smoky flavour can be enjoyed to the full. The meat around the pectoral fins, just behind the gills, is considered the best and, in a sushi shop, is often reserved for special customers. It is used for hand-formed sushi in Japan; some sushi connoisseurs prefer it to tuna. The best choices are those caught using hook and line, or those farmed in closed tanks.

DOVER SOLE
shita birame

The Japanese name means "tongue" – an apt description of this odd-looking fish with its disproportionately small head and tapering tail. It can grow up to 70cm (28in) in length and has a wonderfully delicate flavour and texture. It is available all year round except from April to June, its breeding season. Opt for Dover sole from certified fisheries, which manage their stocks, and avoid choosing immature fish, which will be less than 30cm (12in) long.

133

MAKING SUSHI

SCATTERED SUSHI

chirashi zushi

This is by far the **easiest** type of sushi to prepare. It is widely made across Japan using **regional or seasonal** ingredients but seems relatively unknown in the West. That is a shame, because it is highly **versatile**. Chirashi zushi means "scattered sushi" (rather than shaped), and it might be described as a rice salad. You can **interpret** and **improvise** this style of sushi in many ways – as a one-bowl meal, elegant starter dish, or stylish canapé.

Despite this flexibility, *chirashi zushi* is **traditional** and dates from the early 18th century. It comes in two typical styles: in *Edomae*, or Tokyo-style, slices of sashimi are arranged artistically on a bed of sushi rice and usually served in **individual portions**, while in *Kansai*-style (from the Osaka region), the ingredients are often **cooked and mixed** with sushi rice.

Although making scattered sushi is easy, there are a few points to follow. Resist overloading the rice with your favourite ingredients – **keep it simple**. Don't overmix either, or the rice and fillings could become mushy. Another important point to remember is **presentation** – choose a serving bowl or platter that complements the look of your creation.

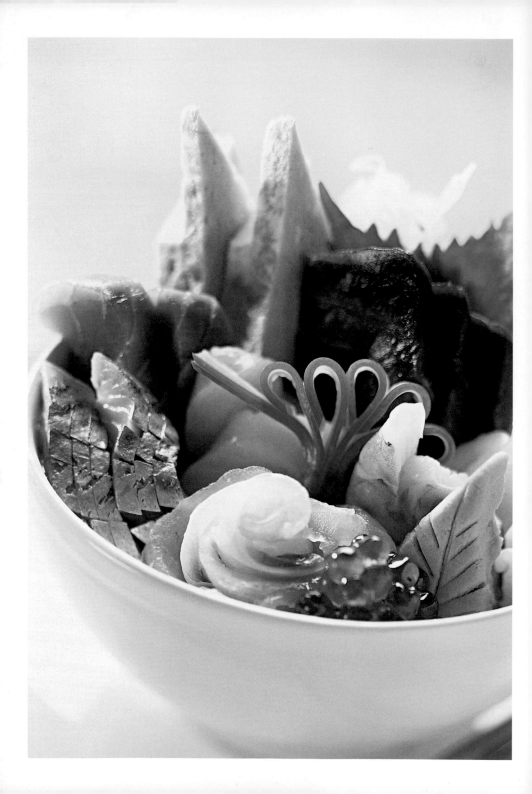

TOKYO-STYLE SUSHI
edomae chirashi zushi

Originally, this dish would have been a simple one-course meal – a bowl of rice topped with a few slices of raw fish and whatever vegetables were cheap and good on the day. It was popular in Edo, which is now Tokyo. There is no strict rule as to what seafood to use – try to combine good colours and textures. Unlike many other scattered sushi, *edomae chirashi zushi* is best served in individual bowls. Arrange the ingredients however you like, but try to mix shapes and colours. To speed assembly, prepare everything beforehand.

SERVES 4 | **PREPARATION TIME** 1 hour, plus sushi rice and ingredient preparation

INGREDIENTS

1 quantity sushi rice (pp.38–41)

1 vinegar-marinated mackerel fillet (pp.100–01) about 120g (4oz), cut into 8 slices

1 rolled Japanese omelette (pp.44–46), cut into 8 strips, 1cm (½in) thick

4 tbsp shredded daikon or cucumber (p.49)

1 baby cucumber, cut into pine branch garnishes (p.50)

4 wasabi paste leaves made with 4 tsp paste (p.51)

1 medium squid body, about 90g (3oz), cleaned (pp.122–23) and cut into 4 strips

4 prepared tiger prawns (pp.118–19)

4 white fish roses made using 120g (4oz) skinless fillet of white fish (p.244)

1 skinless fillet of tuna, about 150g (5oz), cut as for sashimi (pp.96–97) into 12 slices

1 skinless fillet of salmon, about 150g (5oz), cut as for sashimi (pp.96–97) into 8 slices

4 scallops, cut in half

4 perilla leaves or mustard cress, to garnish

4 tsp salmon roe

METHOD

1 Start by preparing the ingredients for assembly. Make the sushi rice, then prepare the mackerel as it will need time to marinate. While the rice is cooling, prepare the omelette, then the daikon and cucumber garnishes and wasabi leaves, and lastly the raw fish and shellfish, to keep them fresh.

CONTINUED ▶

2 Fill each bowl two-thirds full with sushi rice. Place a small, loose ball of shredded daikon or cucumber against one side of each bowl; lean a perilla leaf against it, or use mustard cress.

3 Position 3 slices of tuna and 2 pieces of omelette in front of the perilla leaf or mustard cress.

4 Curl each piece of squid, and place in front of the omelette. Arrange 2 slices of salmon next to the tuna.

Mix colours and textures to create an attractive bowl

5 Make a cut in the back of a prawn so that it folds in half and add it to the arrangement.

6 Arrange 2 slices of mackerel with silver skin showing, 2 scallop halves, and a white fish rose in the bowl.

7 Add a spoonful of salmon roe, and finally, garnish with a wasabi leaf and a cucumber pine branch.

SPICY, SEARED TUNA AND AVOCADO SUSHI BOWL

This recipe captures the free-and-easy appeal of scattered sushi with spicy tuna and plenty of salad vegetables, all served in one bowl like Tokyo-style sushi (see pp.138–41).

SERVES 4 | **PREPARATION TIME** 40 minutes, plus sushi rice and ingredient preparation

INGREDIENTS

4 tuna steaks, each weighing about 100g (3½oz)

2 tbsp sesame oil

1–2 tsp salt

1–2 tsp cayenne pepper

2 tbsp toasted white sesame seeds, plus 2 tsp extra to garnish

1 quantity sushi rice (pp.38–41)

2 avocados, halved, stoned, and peeled

1 large carrot, peeled

½ cucumber

4 spring onions, white parts only, finely sliced lengthways into strips

6 cherry tomatoes, halved

2 tbsp prepared sushi vinegar (p.38)

2 tsp soy sauce

METHOD

1 Preheat a heavy-bottomed griddle pan over a high heat. Brush the tuna steaks with the sesame oil and season with the salt and cayenne pepper, then coat each steak in ½ tbsp of sesame seeds.

2 When the griddle pan is almost smoking hot, sear each tuna steak for 1 minute on each side. (This should leave the tuna raw in the middle.) Remove the tuna from the pan and let it rest for 5 minutes before slicing.

3 Meanwhile, divide the sushi rice into 4 individual bowls. Cut each avocado half into 2–3mm (⅛in) slices, then place your palm over and lightly push down with a twisting motion to create a neat fan of slices. Lift the whole sliced half and place on top of the rice. Using a vegetable peeler, make carrot and cucumber ribbons, each portion weighing about 20g (¾oz), then arrange in each bowl.

4 Cut the tuna into slices 5–8mm (¼in) thick and arrange in each bowl. Add a scattering of finely sliced spring onions and 3 cherry tomato halves per bowl. Drizzle some sushi vinegar and soy sauce on top, and add a sprinkle of toasted sesame seeds to serve.

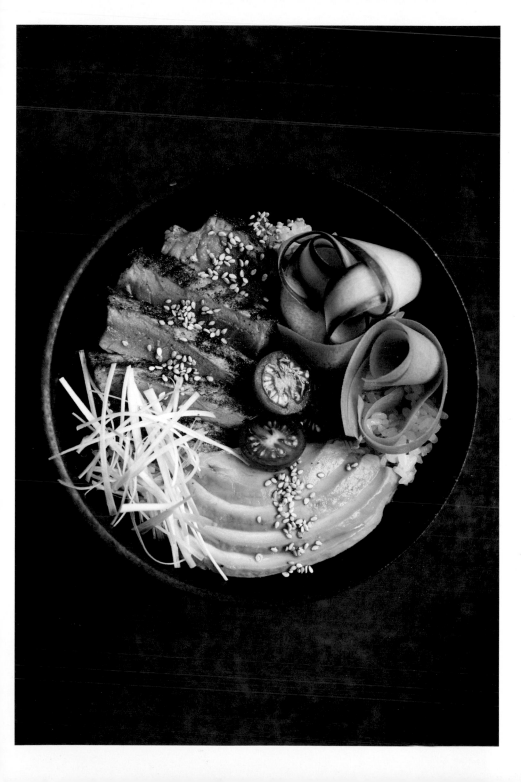

VEGETARIAN SCATTERED SUSHI

gomoku zushi

This is one of the easiest types of sushi to prepare at home. In Japan it is made with the offcuts of whatever vegetables are found in the refrigerator. You could add asparagus to this dish – I've even been known to throw in a handful of frozen peas. It makes an ideal lunch dish, is great for picnics, and can even be served as a light dinner-party starter. Save time by preparing the shiitake mushrooms, kampyo, and tofu pouches in advance.

SERVES 4 | **PREPARATION TIME** 40 minutes, plus sushi rice and ingredient preparation

INGREDIENTS

30g (1oz) mangetout

1 quantity sushi rice (pp.38–41)

4 large seasoned shiitake mushrooms (p.32), thinly sliced

30g (1oz) prepared kampyo (p.31), chopped into 2cm (¾in) lengths

2 seasoned deep-fried tofu pouches (p.162), unseparated, thinly sliced

60g (2oz) lotus root, thinly sliced

1 carrot, cut into flowers (p.48)

3–4 thin Japanese omelettes (p.43)

2 sheets nori seaweed, thinly shredded

METHOD

1 Steam or blanch the mangetout until tender, about 4–5 minutes. Reserve a few whole mangetout to use as a garnish and chop the rest.

2 Spread the rice in the bottom of a large serving dish, or divide between 4 individual bowls. Keep the rice as loose as possible.

3 Scatter the shiitake mushroom slices, the kampyo, and the tofu pouch slices over the rice.

4 Set aside a few slices of lotus root and a few carrot flowers to use as a garnish. Add the remaining lotus root slices, the carrot flowers, and the chopped mangetout.

5 Cut the omelette into fine shreds and scatter over the rice. Garnish with the slices of lotus root and the reserved carrot flowers and mangetout.

6 Sprinkle with the shredded nori just before serving. Add this at the very last minute, otherwise it will go soggy.

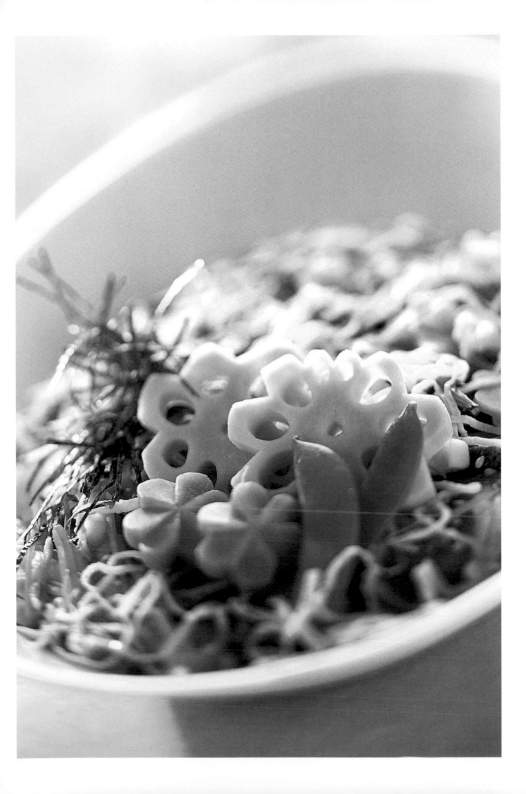

ASPARAGUS AND SCRAMBLED EGG SUSHI

I like to serve this sushi in the spring when asparagus comes into season, but you can make it at any time of year and use whatever green vegetable is in season.

SERVES 4 | **PREPARATION TIME** 40 minutes, plus sushi rice and ingredient preparation

INGREDIENTS

500g (1lb) asparagus, trimmed

1 quantity sushi rice (pp.38–41)

1 quantity scrambled eggs (p.42)

METHOD

1 Steam the asparagus for 2–3 minutes. Reserve the tips to use as a garnish, and chop the stalks into small pea-sized pieces.

2 Mix the sushi rice and chopped asparagus stalks together in a large mixing bowl. Spread the mixture in a large serving dish, or divide between 4 individual bowls.

3 Scatter the scrambled egg over the rice and garnish with the asparagus tips.

MANGETOUT AND VINE TOMATO SUSHI

This is an excellent light lunch in the summer. The combination of slightly crunchy bright green mangetout and sweet, succulent vine tomatoes is quite refreshing.

SERVES 4 | **PREPARATION TIME** 40 minutes, plus sushi rice and ingredient preparation

INGREDIENTS

150g (5oz) mangetout

1 quantity sushi rice (pp.38–41)

150g (5oz) vine tomatoes, deseeded and finely chopped

1 tbsp toasted sesame seeds

METHOD

1 Blanch the mangetout and cool immediately in cold water. Reserve a few whole mangetout to use as a garnish, and cut the remaining ones into thin strips.

2 Mix the sushi rice with the mangetout and chopped tomatoes in a large mixing bowl. Spread the mixture in a large serving dish, or divide between 4 individual bowls.

3 Sprinkle over the toasted sesame seeds and garnish with the reserved mangetout.

Back: Asparagus and scrambled egg sushi　　**Front:** Mangetout and vine tomato sushi

BROCCOLI AND SHREDDED OMELETTE SUSHI

Take care to steam the broccoli only briefly as this retains its vibrant colour and crunchiness. Pickled ginger gives this dish a fresh, lively flavour.

SERVES 4 | **PREPARATION TIME** 40 minutes, plus sushi rice and ingredient preparation

INGREDIENTS

500g (1lb) purple sprouting broccoli, tough stems removed

4 thin omelettes (p.43)

1 quantity sushi rice (pp.38–41)

4 tbsp shredded red or pink pickled ginger

2 tbsp toasted sesame seeds

METHOD

1 Cut the broccoli into small, bite-size pieces. Steam for 2 minutes, then set aside to cool.

2 Stack the omelettes on top of each other and roll up tightly. Finely shred by cutting very thin slices at an angle. Mix the sushi rice, broccoli, and omelette in a large bowl.

3 Transfer the rice mixture to a large serving dish, or divide it between 4 individual serving plates. Place a small mound of ginger on top of the rice. Sprinkle over the sesame seeds before serving.

MUSHROOM AND EGG SUSHI

Mushroom and egg complement each other perfectly in this dish.
Use fresh enoki, shiitake, or oyster mushrooms.

SERVES 4 | **PREPARATION TIME** 40 minutes, plus sushi rice and ingredient preparation

INGREDIENTS

2 tbsp vegetable oil

500g (1lb) mushrooms, sliced into 1cm (½in) strips

1 tbsp soy sauce

1 quantity sushi rice (pp.38–41)

2 tbsp toasted sesame seeds

4 thin omelettes (p.43)

shredded nori, to garnish

METHOD

1 Heat the oil in a large frying pan or wok over a medium-high heat, and stir-fry the mushrooms for 2 minutes. Remove from the heat, add the soy sauce, and stir gently to combine. Drain the mixture of excess liquid using a sieve, then set aside.

2 Combine the sushi rice with the cooked mushrooms and sesame seeds in a large bowl.

3 Transfer the rice mixture to a large serving dish, or divide between 4 individual plates. Cut the omelettes into fine shreds, then sprinkle over the rice. Garnish with the shredded nori just before serving.

Back: Broccoli and shredded omelette sushi   **Front:** Mushroom and egg sushi

SUN-DRIED TOMATO AND MOZZARELLA SUSHI

This quick and easy recipe has an Italian twist, reflecting the way sushi can be embraced and adapted around the world to use local flavours.

SERVES 4 | **PREPARATION TIME** 30 minutes, plus sushi rice and ingredient preparation

INGREDIENTS

1 quantity sushi rice (pp.38–41)

100g (3½oz) sun-dried tomatoes, drained and sliced

175g (6oz) fresh mozzarella cheese, drained and cubed

large bunch of fresh basil leaves, to garnish

METHOD

1 Mix the sushi rice, sun-dried tomatoes, and mozzarella cheese together in a large mixing bowl. If the rice is too cold and solid to mix, gently fold in 1 tbsp Japanese rice vinegar to loosen it.

2 Transfer the rice mixture to a large serving dish, or divide it between 4 individual bowls. Garnish with whole fresh basil leaves and serve.

CRABMEAT, CHILLI, AND LIME SUSHI

This is fusion sushi that combines fresh crab and chillies, two favourites of mine. Vary the amount of chilli to suit your taste and add a little lime juice to help bring the contrasting flavours together. You might find it more economical to buy frozen white crabmeat.

SERVES 4 | **PREPARATION TIME** 40 minutes, plus sushi rice and ingredient preparation

INGREDIENTS

1 quantity sushi rice (pp.38–41)

175g (6oz) white crabmeat

2–4 large red chillies, deseeded and finely chopped

4 sheets nori seaweed

juice of 1 lime

fresh coriander leaves and slices of lime, to garnish

METHOD

1 Combine the sushi rice, crabmeat, and chopped chillies in a large mixing bowl.

2 Trim each sheet of nori to plate size, and lay a square on 4 individual plates.

3 Divide the rice mixture between the individual plates, piling it on top of the nori squares. Squeeze a little lime juice over the rice; garnish with the coriander leaves and slices of lime, and serve.

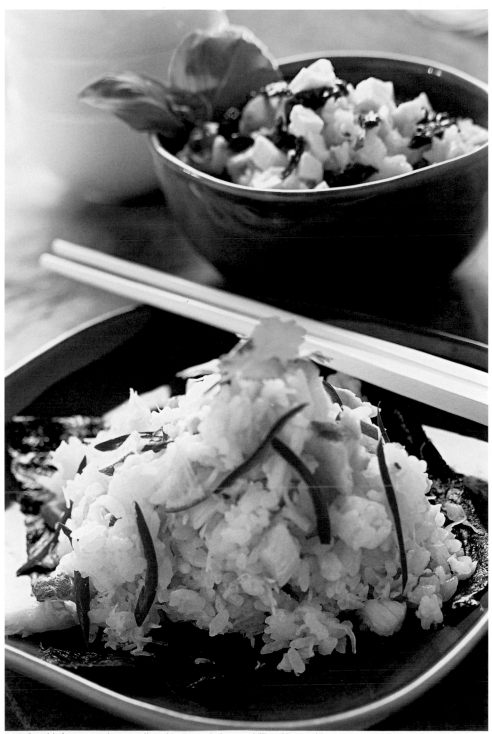

Back: Sun-dried tomato and mozzarella sushi   **Front:** Crabmeat, chilli, and lime sushi

TUNA AND SPRING ONION SUSHI BOWL

In this recipe, tuna is marinated in a soy-based mixture. Known as *tekkadon* in Japan, it is a very popular one-bowl lunch, and is quick and easy to make.

SERVES 4 | **PREPARATION TIME** 30 minutes, plus sushi rice and ingredient preparation

INGREDIENTS

2 tbsp sake

2 tbsp mirin

2 tsp wasabi paste

4 tbsp soy sauce

400g (14oz) tuna, cut into 1cm (½in) thick bite-sized pieces

1 quantity sushi rice (pp.38–41)

2 spring onions, finely sliced diagonally

4 tbsp shredded nori, to garnish

METHOD

1 In a medium-sized bowl, mix the sake, mirin, wasabi paste, and soy sauce to make a marinade. Add the tuna pieces and turn to mix gently so that each piece is well coated. Set aside to marinate for 10–15 minutes.

2 Divide the sushi rice between 4 individual serving bowls. Divide the tuna into 4 equal portions, arrange it on top of the rice, and spoon over the remaining marinade. Sprinkle the spring onions and shredded nori on top of the tuna to serve.

FLAKED SALMON AND ROE SUSHI BOWL

This version of a famous regional specialty from Hokkaido uses readily available cooked salmon flakes instead of the regional salted salmon.

SERVES 4 | **PREPARATION TIME** 20 minutes, plus sushi rice and ingredient preparation

INGREDIENTS

1 quantity sushi rice (pp.38–41)

4 tbsp chopped cornichons

4 tbsp toasted white sesame seeds, plus extra to garnish

200g (7oz) cooked salmon flakes

4 tbsp salmon roe

4 tsp sake

2 tbsp shredded nori, to garnish

METHOD

1 Wet the inside of a large non-reactive mixing bowl with prepared sushi vinegar (p.38), to prevent the sushi rice from sticking to it. Combine the rice, cornichons, sesame seeds, and salmon flakes in the mixing bowl, then divide the mixture between 4 individual bowls.

2 Mix the salmon roe with the sake in a small cup – this makes the roe less sticky. Top each bowl with 1 tbsp of roe mixture, sprinkle with sesame seeds, and garnish with a pile of shredded nori in the centre to serve.

Top: Tuna and spring onion sushi bowl   **Bottom:** Flaked salmon and roe sushi bowl

SEARED BEEF FILLET AND RED ONION SUSHI

This recipe uses the traditional Japanese method for cooking bonito fish, *tataki*, to cook beef, but it works just as well with tuna steak. The beef is briefly seared to seal in the flavour while the centre remains almost rare. Submerging the seared beef in ice-cold water instantly halts the cooking process and also washes away excess fat. You can save time by preparing up to step 5 in advance. This is a robust dish that should be enjoyed with a full-bodied red wine.

SERVES 4 | **PREPARATION TIME** 1 hour 15 minutes, plus sushi rice and ingredient preparation

INGREDIENTS

1 medium red onion, peeled and halved

500g (1lb) beef fillet

salt and freshly ground black pepper

1 tbsp vegetable oil

100ml (3½ fl oz) sake

100ml (3½ fl oz) soy sauce

1 quantity sushi rice (pp.38–41)

2 spring onions, finely sliced, to garnish

chilli daikon relish (p.34)

METHOD

1 Cut the onion into thin slices and place in a bowl of cold water. Set aside to soak. Pat dry the beef fillet with kitchen paper. Rub salt and pepper into it, and set aside to season for 30 minutes.

CONTINUED ▶

2 Heat the oil in a large heavy-bottomed frying pan and sear the beef until brown, about 2 minutes on each side.

3 The surface of the beef should be well browned, but the inside should be raw. However, you can cook the meat for longer if you prefer it less rare.

4 Transfer the beef to a bowl of iced water and leave to stand for 10 minutes. Combine the sake and soy in a shallow dish.

5 Wipe the beef dry with kitchen paper and transfer to the dish of sake and soy mixture. Set aside to marinate for at least 10–15 minutes.

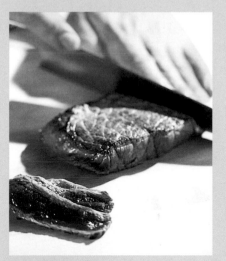

6 Remove the beef from the marinade and pat dry with kitchen paper. Cut into 5mm (¼in) thick slices, or as thinly as possible.

7 Fill each bowl two-thirds full with sushi rice, and top with the slices of beef. Drizzle 1 tbsp of the marinade over the beef slices in each bowl.

8 Drain the onion slices and use to garnish. Sprinkle over the spring onions, and serve with chilli daikon relish.

157

BROCCOLI AND EGG SUSHI CANAPÉS

Scattered sushi is highly versatile and can be served in many different ways.
Here, witloof chicory, or Belgian endive, leaves are used as edible serving vessels.

MAKES 25–30 canapés | **PREPARATION TIME** 40 minutes, plus sushi rice and ingredient preparation

INGREDIENTS

200g (7oz) sprouting broccoli

½ quantity sushi rice
(pp.38–41)

1 quantity scrambled
eggs (p.42)

1 tbsp toasted white
sesame seeds

1 tbsp toasted black
sesame seeds

6 heads of witloof chicory,
25–30 outer leaves separated

METHOD

1 Chop the broccoli into bite-sized pieces and blanch
for 1 minute in salted boiling water. Drain the broccoli,
then plunge into a bowl of iced water to cool and preserve
the colour. Drain again and pat dry with kitchen paper,
then set aside.

2 Wet the inside of a non-reactive mixing bowl with
prepared sushi vinegar (p.38), to prevent the sushi rice
from sticking to it. Add the rice, broccoli, scrambled eggs,
and sesame seeds, and mix to combine. Using a serving
spoon, shape the rice mixture into bite-sized nuggets and
put each nugget in a chicory leaf to serve.

POMEGRANATE AND PRAWN SUSHI CANAPÉS

Here is another idea for a sushi canapé using the leaves of Little Gem lettuce
to serve a tasty pomegranate and prawn filling. It couldn't be easier to assemble.

MAKES 30–35 canapés | **PREPARATION TIME** 40 minutes, plus sushi rice and ingredient preparation

INGREDIENTS

1 pomegranate

½ quantity sushi rice
(pp.38–41)

200g (7oz) cooked prawns,
roughly chopped

6 heads of Little Gem lettuce,
30–35 outer leaves separated

a few sprigs of coriander
leaves, to garnish

METHOD

1 Roll the pomegranate on a work surface to loosen the
seeds, then score around the middle using a knife. Tear
open into two halves. Over a bowl, strike the back of each
half with wooden spoon until all the seeds fall out.

2 Wet the inside of a non-reactive mixing bowl with
prepared sushi vinegar (p.38), to prevent the sushi rice
from sticking to it. Add the rice, pomegranate seeds, and
prawns, and mix to combine. Using a serving spoon, shape
the rice mixture into bite-sized nuggets and put each nugget
in a lettuce leaf "boat". Garnish with coriander, and serve.

Top: Broccoli and egg sushi canapés   **Second from top:** Pomegranate and prawn sushi canapés

STUFFED SUSHI

inari zushi

This form of sushi uses **cooked ingredients** such as thin omelettes, cabbage leaves, or deep-fried tofu as wrapping material for sushi rice and other cooked ingredients. Vegetarian stuffed sushi, especially the traditional *inari zushi*, which is made with delicious pouches of seasoned, deep-fried tofu, is great to take on a picnic – it is **easy to transport** and tends not to spoil quickly.

The Japanese prepare stuffed sushi at home and eat the **tasty little parcels** under cherry trees in spring, which are famous for their beautiful, fragrant blossom. The fillings can vary from simple plain sushi rice mixed with a few chopped **fresh herbs** to whatever **seasonal ingredients** are available. There are no strict rules as to what you can or cannot use – I have included a recipe for one of my personal favourites, stuffed squid sushi. Because most types of stuffed sushi can be prepared up to six hours in advance, it also makes a **convenient** party food. The sushi sandwich, or *onigirazu*, is a new type of sushi that is a favourite in Japanese lunch boxes.

STUFFED TOFU PARCELS
inari zushi

Highly portable, *inari zushi* is great for a lunchbox or picnic food. The sushi rice filling is wrapped in deep-fried tofu, or *abura age*, which can be bought from Japanese shops and has a distinctive sweet-and-savoury flavour. You can try adding other flavourings to the rice, such as chopped perilla leaves or lemon zest.

MAKES 12 parcels | **PREPARATION TIME** 1 hour, plus sushi rice and ingredient preparation

INGREDIENTS

**For the
tofu pouches**

6 pieces *abura age*, or deep-fried tofu

½ quantity dashi stock (p.47)

3 tbsp sugar

4–5 tbsp soy sauce

2 tbsp sake

2 tbsp mirin

For the stuffed sushi

1 quantity sushi rice (pp.38–41)

2 tbsp toasted sesame seeds

6 seasoned shiitake mushrooms (p.32), very finely sliced

METHOD

1 To make the tofu pouches, cut each piece of deep-fried tofu in half and open it up (see below). Season the pouches by simmering them with the remaining ingredients in a saucepan for 15–20 minutes. Drain in a colander.

2 Mix the sushi rice with the sesame seeds and mushrooms in a large mixing bowl. Carefully spoon the filling into each tofu pouch until it is half full. Use your fingers to loosely pack the filling, but make sure you don't overfill the pouch. Make a parcel by tucking one edge of the tofu pouch under the filling, then folding the other edge over the top. Repeat with the other pouches to make 12 parcels.

HOW TO MAKE AND SEASON TOFU POUCHES

To make it easier to open, roll a chopstick over the tofu first. In a colander, douse with boiling water to remove oils.

Simmer the pouches with the other ingredients over a low heat until most of the liquid has reduced.

STUFFED SQUID SUSHI

ika zushi

Here, squid is first cooked in a sweet vinegar mix, *amazu*, and then stuffed with
a mixture of seasoned rice and vegetables. Experiment with different stuffings,
but as *ika zushi* is always served sliced, use vegetables such as green beans,
carrots, cucumbers, and chillies that add colour.

SERVES 4 | **PREPARATION TIME** 1 hour, plus sushi rice and ingredient preparation

INGREDIENTS

For the amazu

3 tbsp Japanese rice vinegar

1 tbsp sugar

1 tsp salt

For the stuffed squid

2 medium squid with
tentacles, about 300g (10oz)
each, cleaned and body
intact (pp.122–23)

1 tbsp soy sauce

60g (2oz) green beans,
trimmed

1 quantity sushi rice
(pp.38–41)

5cm (2in) piece fresh
ginger, peeled and grated

5 perilla leaves, chopped,
or 2 tbsp chopped fresh
coriander leaves

METHOD

1 Mix all the ingredients for the amazu together in
a small bowl. Add to the squid with the soy sauce
in a non-aluminium pan. Cook gently for 2–3 minutes.

CONTINUED ▶

2 Drain the squid and set to one side. Once cool enough to handle, chop the tentacles. Steam or blanch the green beans until tender, about 2–3 minutes, then chop into small pea-sized pieces.

3 Mix the sushi rice with the chopped green beans, grated ginger, chopped tentacles, and chopped perilla leaves or coriander in a bowl.

4 Spoon the rice mixture into each of the marinated squid bodies.

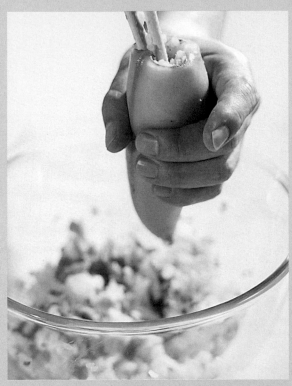

5 Gently pack the filling into the squid with a pair of cooking chopsticks or a spoon. Set aside to stand at room temperature for between 30 minutes and 1 hour to allow the flavours to develop.

Refresh solid, hard-to-mix rice with a little sushi vinegar

6 Use a sharp knife dipped in water to slice the stuffed squid into 2cm (¾in) thick rounds. Arrange on a plate and serve.

Top: Omelette purse   **Bottom:** Omelette parcel (p.170)

OMELETTE PURSES
chakin zushi

Both omelette purses and parcels (see pp.170–71) make elegant starter dishes. Omelette makes a colourful wrapping material, and here each stuffed purse is tied with a bright green coriander stalk. You will need a 24cm (9½in) frying pan.

MAKES 8 purses | **PREPARATION TIME** 1 hour 30 minutes, plus sushi rice and ingredient preparation

INGREDIENTS

1 quantity sushi rice (pp.38–41)

4 seasoned shiitake mushrooms (p.32), thinly sliced

2 tbsp toasted sesame seeds

8 thin Japanese omelettes (p.43)

8 coriander or flat-leaf parsley stalks, leaves removed, 15cm (6in) long

METHOD

1 Mix the sushi rice with the shiitake mushrooms and sesame seeds in a bowl. Place an omelette on a clean surface or chopping board and spoon about 2 tbsp rice stuffing into the middle of it.

Be careful not to tear the wrapping by overstuffing

2 Run the back of a knife along the coriander or flat-leaf parsley stalk to tenderize it. Gather up the edges of the omelette and tie together with the stalk. Repeat to make 8 purses.

OMELETTE PARCELS

fukusa zushi

A fukusa is a small handkerchief used in the traditional Japanese tea ceremony. It is folded in different ways as part of the ceremonial performance. Here, a thin Japanese omelette is folded into a parcel and stuffed with a filling of rice, shiitake mushrooms, and sesame seeds. This sushi is popular with my vegetarian friends. You will need a 28cm (11in) non-stick frying pan to make the omelettes.

MAKES 8 parcels | **PREPARATION TIME** 1 hour 20 minutes, plus sushi rice and ingredient preparation

INGREDIENTS

1 quantity sushi rice
(pp.38–41)

8 seasoned shiitake
mushrooms (p.32),
thinly sliced

2 tbsp toasted sesame seeds

8 thin Japanese omelettes
(p.43)

8 strips of prepared kampyo
(p.31), 12cm (5in) long
or 8 coriander stalks,
leaves removed

Cold rice will be hard to mix, so don't refrigerate it

METHOD

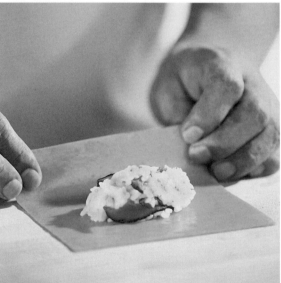

1 Mix the sushi rice with the shiitake mushrooms and sesame seeds in a bowl. Place an omelette on a clean surface or chopping board and cut the edges off it to form roughly a 20cm (8in) square. Spoon about 2 tbsp rice stuffing into the middle of the omelette square.

2 Position the omelette so that one corner faces you. Fold this lower corner over the filling to meet the top corner.

3 Then one after the other, fold in the side corners to meet at the centre.

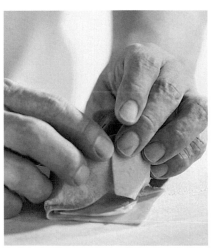

4 Now fold the omelette over the top corner to form a neat, rectangular parcel.

5 Use a strip of seasoned kampyo or a coriander stalk, tenderized by running the back of a knife along it, to tie the parcel. Repeat to make 8 parcels.

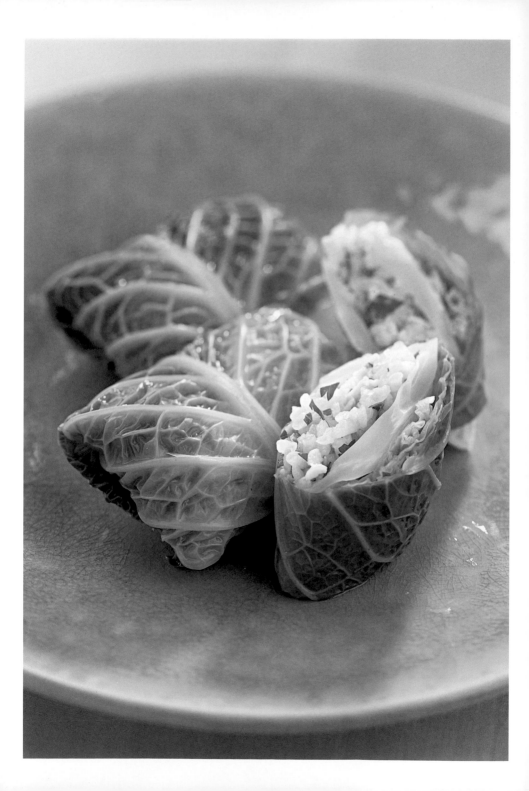

SAVOY CABBAGE LEAVES WITH HERB AND EGG RICE

The bright green colour and crinkled texture of Savoy cabbage make it an interesting wrapping material. The leaves are blanched very briefly then immersed in cold water, which helps them to retain their colour. Be sure to pat any excess water off the leaves, otherwise the stuffing can become soggy. Use the same technique to fold these parcels as for omelette parcels (see pp.170–71).

MAKES 8 parcels | **PREPARATION TIME** 45 minutes, plus sushi rice and ingredient preparation

INGREDIENTS

8 large Savoy cabbage leaves

½ quantity sushi rice (pp.38–41)

1oz (30g) mixed herbs such as flat-leaf parsley, coriander, spring onions, or mint, finely chopped

1 quantity scrambled eggs (p.42)

2 tbsp toasted sesame seeds

8 wooden skewers or toothpicks

METHOD

1 Cut out and discard the thick stems at the base of each cabbage leaf. Bring a large pan of water to the boil, and blanch the cabbage leaves for about 2 minutes. Remove and immerse immediately in a bowl of cold water. Pat any excess water off the leaves.

2 Mix the sushi rice with the herbs, scrambled eggs, and sesame seeds in a bowl.

3 Place a cabbage leaf on a clean surface or chopping board and put 1 tbsp rice mixture in the middle of it.

4 Fold over the near and far edges of the leaf so that they overlap in the middle. Then fold the other opposite edges over to make a parcel.

5 Secure the parcel by piercing it with a small wooden skewer or toothpick. Repeat the process to make 8 parcels. Be sure to remind people to remove the skewers or toothpicks before eating.

If the wrapping tears, reduce the stuffing and try again

SUSHI SANDWICHES

onigirazu

This innovative take on traditional onigiri (rice ball) contains colourful fillings in layers of rice and a nori wrapping. *Onigirazu* is perfect for a lunchbox or picnic, but use cooked or marinated fish if you won't be able to keep raw fish chilled.

MAKES 4 sandwiches | **PREPARATION TIME** 30 minutes, plus sushi rice and ingredient preparation

INGREDIENTS

4 nori sheets

1 quantity sushi rice (pp.38–41)

½ red pepper, cut into thin strips

½ green pepper, cut into thin strips

200g (7oz) skinless salmon fillet, cut into large sashimi-size pieces (pp.96–97)

1 thin Japanese omelette (p.43)

METHOD

1 Place a nori sheet shiny-side down with one corner pointing north. Place one-eighth of the sushi rice (about 70–80g/2½ oz in weight) in the centre of the nori sheet. Shape it into an 8cm (3in) square using the back of a serving spoon, and gently press down the surface (see below).

2 Layer one-quarter of the strips of pepper on top of the rice square, alternating the colours, then add one-quarter of the salmon. Cut the omelette into quarters and place one quartered piece over the salmon.

3 Place another one-eighth of rice on top of the filling, shaping as before. Fold two corners of the nori to the centre, then fold the remaining corners to close (see below).

4 Wrap the rice sandwich with cling film and set aside to allow the nori to settle while you make 3 more onigirazu. Cut the onigirazu in half with a moistened knife to serve.

HOW TO BUILD LAYERS

On a nori sheet with one corner facing north, place a square of rice, leaving room at the sides.

Layer your fillings in the same direction so you get a cross-section when you cut the sandwich.

Place another rice square over the fillings, then fold the corners of the nori in to close the sandwich.

SEARED DUCK BREAST IN RICE PAPER PARCELS

Pan-fried duck breast is wrapped in Thai rice paper and drizzled with traditional Japanese teriyaki sauce in this innovative recipe. Teriyaki sauce can be bought ready-made, but it's worth taking a little extra time to make this delicious version yourself. Serve it as a dipping sauce or keep it for up to one week in a sealed container in the refrigerator.

MAKES 4 parcels | **PREPARATION TIME** 45 minutes, plus sushi rice and ingredient preparation

INGREDIENTS

For the savoury teriyaki sauce

60ml (2fl oz) mirin

60ml (2fl oz) soy sauce

2 tbsp sugar

5cm (2in) piece fresh ginger, peeled

5cm (2in) piece carrot, peeled

1 medium onion, peeled and halved

For the parcels

1 duck breast

4 round sheets rice paper

½ quantity sushi rice (pp.38–41)

½ cucumber, cut into thin strips

METHOD

1 Put all the ingredients for the teriyaki sauce in a small saucepan and heat gently. Stir until the sugar dissolves, then leave to simmer until the sauce has thickened and reduced by one-third, about 20 minutes. Meanwhile, prepare the duck.

CONTINUED ▶

2 Use a sharp knife to cut a series of shallow slits in the skin of the duck breast to help the fat drain away.

3 Heat a heavy-bottomed frying pan over a medium heat. Cook the duck breast skin-side down until brown and crispy, about 5–10 minutes. Turn over and cook for a further 3–5 minutes.

4 Remove the duck from the heat and plunge into a bowl of boiling hot water, or pour over boiling water to wash off excess fat. Remove from the water and set aside to cool to room temperature.

5 Fill a baking tray with warm water, lay in the sheets of rice paper, and soak until soft, about 2–3 minutes. Remove and drain on kitchen paper. Cut the duck into 5mm (¼in) thick slices.

6 Spread the rice paper on a clean surface or chopping board. Put 1 large tbsp rice in the centre and flatten slightly with the back of a spoon.

7 Add 2–3 slices of duck and a few thin strips of cucumber.

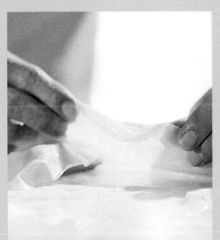

8 To wrap, bring the bottom edge of the rice paper over the filling, then fold in the sides. Continue to wrap to make a small parcel.

9 To serve, cut the parcel diagonally and arrange on a serving plate. Strain the teriyaki sauce and drizzle over the parcels.

PRESSED SUSHI
oshi zushi

Oshi zushi, or pressed sushi, is the **oldest** of today's sushi types, and the one that most closely resembles its ancestor. *Nare zushi*, the ancient form of sushi, involved **packing** fish and cooked rice **tightly** into a barrel or wooden press in order to let the rice slowly ferment and preserve the fish. While modern sushi is no longer a method of preservation, pressed sushi retains the practice of **compacting the rice and toppings** into a mould. Today, pressed sushi is made widely across Japan. There are many **regional specialities**, of which the most famous is *battera*, or marinated mackerel pressed sushi (see pp.182–85), from the city of Osaka.

Traditionally, pressed sushi is made in **box-like** wooden moulds, but they are not a prerequisite. We have used a 15 x 7.5 x 5cm (6 x 3 x 2in) wooden mould for most recipes in this section, but you can easily **improvise with alternative moulds** that you may already have in your kitchen – cooking rings, cookie cutters, or even small coffee cups for making individual portions, or a small cake tin to form a larger sushi "cake" that you can cut into pieces.

MARINATED MACKEREL PRESSED SUSHI

battera

This is one of the most well-known types of pressed sushi. This recipe (and all the recipes from pp.186–91) uses a wooden mould measuring 15 x 7.5 x 5cm (6 x 3 x 2in). Soak the mould in water for about 15 minutes with a weight on top to stop it floating – this prevents the rice from sticking to it. You can prepare as far as step 7 up to six hours in advance.

MAKES 6 pieces | **PREPARATION TIME** 30 minutes, plus sushi rice and ingredient preparation

INGREDIENTS

1 marinated mackerel fillet, weighing about 150g (5oz) (pp.100–101)

1–2 tsp wasabi paste

½ quantity sushi rice (pp.38–41)

METHOD

Soak the mould well beforehand to prevent the rice sticking

1 Trim the mackerel fillet so it is as thin and flat as possible. The offcuts can be used to fill gaps in the mould, so don't discard them.

CONTINUED ▶

2 Cut the fillet to fit the base of the mould, and lay it skin-side down inside the box. Fill any gaps with smaller pieces of mackerel.

3 Cover the bottom of the mould with a patchwork of fillet cuts. Spread a few dabs of wasabi over the mackerel.

4 Add the sushi rice to the mould – it should be about two-thirds full – and use your fingers to pack it down evenly over the mackerel fillets.

5 Put the lid on the mould and press it down firmly to compact the rice.

6 With both thumbs on the lid of the mould, holding it in place, lift off the sides. Then take the lid off and carefully turn the mould over onto a chopping board, so the mackerel is on top.

Use a wet knife to release the rice block if it is stuck

7 Remove the base of the mould. If preparing in advance, wrap the block in cling film and store in a cool place for up to 6 hours, but don't refrigerate.

8 Dip a sharp knife in water, wiping off the excess, and cut the block of sushi in half. Cut each half into 3 equal-sized pieces to make 6 pieces, and serve with pickled ginger.

OMELETTE AND MUSTARD CRESS SUSHI

This simple recipe uses the classic combination of egg and cress. Make sure you buy proper cress – not rape seedlings, the bland supermarket substitute.

MAKES 6 pieces | **PREPARATION TIME** 45 minutes, plus sushi rice and ingredient preparation

INGREDIENTS

2 thin Japanese omelettes (p.43)

½ quantity sushi rice (pp.38–41)

2 cartons mustard cress

METHOD

1 Line the base of a wet sushi mould with omelette. Add the sushi rice, put the lid on, and press gently to compact the rice so that the mould is two-thirds full.

2 Unmould the rice and egg block, and use a knife dipped in water to cut it into 6 equal-sized pieces.

3 Trim the root ends off the cress and top each piece of sushi with a small peppery bunch of cress.

ASPARAGUS AND RED PEPPER SUSHI

Here, the sushi mould is used to shape the rice, and the toppings are added later and arranged in a criss-cross pattern.

MAKES 6 pieces | **PREPARATION TIME** 40 minutes, plus sushi rice and ingredient preparation

INGREDIENTS

1 large red pepper

12 small asparagus spears

½ quantity sushi rice (pp.38–41)

METHOD

1 Grill the red pepper whole until the skin blackens. Put it in a bowl, cover with cling film, and set aside to cool. Meanwhile, steam or blanch the asparagus until tender, about 4 minutes, then plunge into a bowl of ice-cold water.

2 Peel the skin off the red pepper and discard the seeds and the pith. Slice into thin strips. Place the sushi rice in a wet mould, put the lid on, and press gently to compact the rice so that the mould is two-thirds full.

3 Unmould the rice block and cut it into 6 equal-sized pieces using a wet knife. Cut the asparagus stalks to the length of the rice blocks. Arrange them in a row on the rice and make a criss-cross pattern on top with the pepper.

Back: Omelette and mustard cress sushi   **Front:** Asparagus and red pepper sushi

AVOCADO AND SHIITAKE MUSHROOM SUSHI

This recipe combines eastern and western ingredients in a simple and light sushi. The vinegar in the rice balances the high oil content of the avocado.

MAKES 6 pieces | **PREPARATION TIME** 30 minutes, plus sushi rice and ingredient preparation

INGREDIENTS

1 ripe avocado, sliced

½ quantity sushi rice (pp.38–41)

6 seasoned shiitake mushrooms (p.32), sliced

METHOD

1 Line the base of a wet sushi mould with the avocado slices, then add the sushi rice. Put the lid on the mould, and press gently to compact the rice.

2 Unmould the rice and avocado block, and use a knife dipped in water to cut it into 6 equal-sized pieces.

3 Top each piece of sushi with the shiitake mushroom slices, trimming them to fit the rice blocks.

SMOKED SALMON AND CUCUMBER SUSHI

The skill is in arranging the strips of salmon and cucumber. This sushi looks impressive but takes practice to perfect.

MAKES 6 pieces | **PREPARATION TIME** 30 minutes, plus sushi rice and ingredient preparation

INGREDIENTS

100g (3½oz) smoked salmon, cut into strips

15cm (6in) piece cucumber, cut lengthways into thin strips

½ quantity sushi rice (pp.38–41)

METHOD

1 Trim the salmon and cucumber strips so that they fit the mould exactly when placed diagonally in it. Line the base of the wet sushi mould with alternating diagonal strips of smoked salmon and cucumber.

2 Add the sushi rice, then put the lid on the mould, and press gently to compact it.

3 Unmould the rice, salmon, and cucumber block, and use a knife dipped in water to cut it into 6 equal-sized pieces.

Back: Avocado and shiitake mushroom sushi   **Front:** Smoked salmon and cucumber sushi

SEA BASS AND PERILLA LEAF SUSHI

The chilli garnish gives a fiery boost to this delicate sushi. Try to cut the sea bass thinly enough for the green of the perilla leaf to show through the translucent fish.

MAKES 6 pieces | **PREPARATION TIME** 30 minutes, plus sushi rice and ingredient preparation

INGREDIENTS

90–120g (3–4oz) sea bass fillet, thinly sliced (pp.96–97)

about 10 perilla leaves

½ quantity sushi rice (pp.38–41)

1 hot red chilli, cut into thin rounds, to garnish

METHOD

1 Line the bottom of a wet sushi mould with a thin layer of sea bass. Add a thin layer of perilla leaves.

2 Add the sushi rice, put the lid on the mould, and press gently to compact the rice.

3 Unmould the sea bass, perilla leaf, and rice block, and use a knife dipped in water to cut it into 6 equal-sized pieces. Garnish each piece of sushi with a couple of slices of red chilli.

SHIITAKE MUSHROOM AND ZASAI SUSHI

This Chinese-inspired sushi uses zasai, a pickled vegetable with dark green knobbly skin and a crunchy texture. It can be found packaged in jars or tins in any South-east Asian food shop.

MAKES 6 pieces | **PREPARATION TIME** 30 minutes, plus sushi rice and ingredient preparation

INGREDIENTS

100g (3½oz) pickled zasai root

½ quantity sushi rice (pp.38–41)

8 seasoned shiitake mushrooms (p.32), sliced

METHOD

1 Soak the zasai in water for about 1 hour, then drain and cut into thin slices. Line the bottom of a wet sushi mould with the slices of zasai.

2 Fill the mould half-full with sushi rice, then add a layer of shiitake mushroom slices. Add the remaining rice to the mould, put the lid on, and press gently to compact the rice.

3 Unmould the zasai, mushroom, and rice block, and use a knife dipped in water to cut the block into 6 equal-sized pieces.

Left: Sea bass and perilla leaf sushi   **Right:** Shiitake mushroom and zasai sushi

SCALLOP TARTARE PRESSED SUSHI

Instead of a traditional mould, this recipe uses a 7 x 4cm (3 x 1¾in) cooking ring.
Sushi vinegar is used here as a sweet-sour marinade that semi-cures the scallops.

SERVES 4 | **PREPARATION TIME** 1 hour, plus sushi rice and ingredient preparation

INGREDIENTS

8 tbsp sushi vinegar (p.38)

4 tbsp sugar

2 tbsp light soy sauce

1 large red chilli, deseeded
and finely minced

200g (7oz) scallops (without
roe), thinly sliced

½ quantity sushi rice
(pp.38–41)

30cm (12in) piece cucumber

purple shiso leaves (optional)

METHOD

1 Mix the first 4 ingredients in a non-reactive bowl, add the
scallops, and leave to marinade for 30 minutes.

2 Place a wet cooking ring on a serving plate and fill with
one-quarter of the sushi rice. Gently flatten the rice using
the back of a spoon, then remove the ring. Repeat to make
4 rice cylinders.

3 Use a vegetable peeler to make 8 cucumber ribbons,
each 23–25cm (9–10in) long. Wrap a ribbon around each
rice cylinder, then a second above it to form a raised wall to
hold the scallops. Drain the scallops and arrange them on
the rice. Garnish with shiso leaves, if using, and serve.

SMOKED SALMON PRESSED SUSHI WITH ROE

This elegant, modern version of pressed sushi makes a stylish starter. You will
need a 7 x 4cm (3 x 1¾in) cooking ring to use as a mould.

SERVES 4 | **PREPARATION TIME** 30 minutes, plus sushi rice and ingredient preparation

INGREDIENTS

200g (7oz) smoked
salmon slices

½ quantity sushi rice
(pp.38–41)

2 tsp wasabi paste

4 tbsp salmon roe

2 tsp sake

mustard cress (optional)

METHOD

1 Using the cooking ring, stamp out 4 circular pieces of
smoked salmon and set aside. Reserve the offcuts.

2 Follow Step 2 in the scallop recipe (above) to make 4 rice
cylinders. Spread each with ½ tsp wasabi and top with a
salmon circle. Cut the salmon offcuts into strips, and roll into
4 rose shapes (see p.244). Place on top of the salmon circles.

3 Mix the salmon roe with the sake and spoon over the
sushi. Garnish with mustard cress, if using, and serve.

Back: Scallop tartare pressed sushi   **Front:** Smoked salmon pressed sushi with roe

ROLLED SUSHI

maki zushi

The perfect canapé or dinner-party starter, rolled sushi is probably the **most recognizable** type of sushi. It consists of rice and fish, vegetables, or omelette rolled into a cylinder with **nori** seaweed around it, so it is also called *nori maki*. There are **many types** of rolled sushi: thin rolls, *hoso maki*, contain a single ingredient such as tuna or cucumber; thick rolls, *futo maki*, have several different fillings and combine a **variety of flavours**, colours, and textures; inside-out rolls, *uramaki*, have rice on the outside and nori on the inside; and hand-rolled sushi, *temaki zushi*, are cornet-shaped.

Once prepared, sushi rolls with nori on the outside should be eaten straight away to enjoy the **crisp texture** of the nori in contrast with the softer rice and fillings. If left too long, the nori will absorb moisture from the rice, become soggy, and split. Inside-out rolls, on the other hand, are more forgiving and suitable for making in advance. Rolling sushi takes **a little bit of practice**, so don't be disheartened if your first rolls are not perfect. Follow the step-by-step instructions and you will soon master the technique. Just remember to have the rice and other ingredients **ready-prepared** before you start rolling.

THIN ROLL SUSHI
hoso maki zushi

This is believed to be the original form of rolled sushi and uses a single filling such as tuna, cucumber, or seasoned kampyo. Use whatever filling you prefer, but keep it simple. Once you have mastered thin roll sushi, the other varieties are easy. This elegant bite-size sushi makes wonderful finger food and is a guaranteed hit as a dinner party starter.

MAKES 48 pieces | **PREPARATION TIME** 45 minutes, plus sushi rice and ingredient preparation

INGREDIENTS

For the vinegared water

1–2 tbsp rice vinegar

250ml (8fl oz) water

For the sushi rolls

4 sheets nori seaweed

1 quantity sushi rice (pp.38–41)

wasabi paste

1 skinless fillet of tuna, about 120g (4oz), cut into pencil-thick strips (pp.96–97)

½ cucumber, cut into 1cm (½in) square strips

½ quantity rolled Japanese omelette (pp.44–46), cut into 1cm (½in) square strips

METHOD

1 Mix the ingredients for the vinegared water in a small bowl and set aside. Lay a sushi rolling mat on your work surface. Fold a sheet of nori in half across the grain, and pinch along the folded edge to break it in two. Place a halved sheet along the edge of the rolling mat with the shiny, smooth side facing downwards. Dip your hands in the vinegared water to prevent the rice from sticking to them. Take a handful of rice about 70–75g (2½oz) in weight and form it into a log shape.

CONTINUED ▶

2 Place the rice in the centre of the sheet of nori and use the tips of your fingers to spread it evenly over it. Leave about a 1cm (½in) margin of nori along the edge furthest from you.

3 If using a fish filling, dab a thin line of wasabi paste across the centre of the rice. Don't overdo the wasabi – it should complement the flavour of the sushi, not overpower it.

4 Arrange a strip of tuna (or cucumber or omelette) on top of the wasabi. You may need to use 2–3 short pieces, but line them up close to each other with no gaps between them. Lift up the edge of the mat closest to you, and slowly roll away from you in a smooth movement.

5 Roll the mat over so that the top edge of the nori meets the edge of the rice. You need to keep a gentle pressure on the roll to keep it neatly compacted.

6 You should be able to see the strip of nori not covered by rice. Gently shape the length of the roll using both hands and applying even pressure.

7 Lift the edge of the mat slightly and push the roll forward a little so that the uncovered strip of nori seals the roll. The moisture from the rice acts as an adhesive. Push in any stray grains of rice to tidy the ends. Set aside in a cool place – but not the refrigerator – while you make more.

Reposition any off-centre fillings with your fingers

8 Dip a cloth or tea towel in the vinegared water, use it to moisten a sharp knife, and cut each roll in half. Moisten the knife with the cloth between each cutting. Place the two halves next to each other and cut them twice to make 6 equal bite-sized pieces. Arrange on a serving plate and serve immediately.

Other recipes
Try making thin roll sushi with 120g (4oz) skinless fillet of salmon, cut into pencil-thick strips (pp.96–97); 120g (4oz) crabmeat; or 1 medium carrot, cut into 1cm (½in) square strips and lightly steamed.

THICK ROLL SUSHI
futo maki zushi

Because of their colourful assortment of fillings, *futo maki* are also known as *date maki* or "dandy rolls". The rolling technique is similar to thin rolls, but these larger rolls use a whole nori sheet instead of half of one. Experiment with different combinations of fillings to create colourful patterns, but prepare all the fillings before you start assembling the rolls. Ideally, eat them as soon as you can.

MAKES 24 pieces | **PREPARATION TIME** 45 minutes, plus sushi rice and ingredient preparation

INGREDIENTS

For the vinegared water

1–2 tbsp rice vinegar

250ml (8fl oz) water

For the sushi rolls

3 sheets nori seaweed

1 quantity sushi rice
(pp.38–41)

1 carrot, cut into pencil-thick
strips and steamed

30g (1oz) green beans,
trimmed and lightly steamed

30g (1oz) seasoned shiitake
mushrooms (p.32)

30g (1oz) prepared
kampyo (p.31)

1 rolled Japanese omelette
(pp.44–46), cut into 1cm
(½in) strips

METHOD

1 Mix the ingredients for the vinegared water in a small bowl and set aside. Lay a bamboo rolling mat on your work surface and place a sheet of nori shiny-side down on it. Dip your hands in the vinegared water, form two handfuls of rice, each about 100g (3½oz) in weight, into log shapes and place at the centre of the nori.

CONTINUED ▶

2 Spread the rice evenly across the whole width of the nori, leaving a 4cm (1¾in) margin on the edge of the nori furthest from you.

3 Lay one-third of the carrot strips in the centre of the rice with one-third of the green beans and one-third of the shiitake mushrooms on either side. Arrange one-third of the kampyo next to the green beans and one-third of the omelette strips alongside the shiitake mushrooms.

4 Place your thumbs under the rolling mat and lift the near edge of the mat with your thumbs and index fingers. Hold the fillings in place with the rest of your fingers.

5 Holding a small flap at the top of the mat, bring the near side of the roll over so that it covers the fillings.

6 Bring the rolling mat down to meet the strip of nori and gently squeeze along the length of the roll to tuck in the near edge of the nori.

7 Lift the front edge of the mat slightly with one hand and use the other to gently push the roll forward so that the strip of nori not covered by rice seals the roll.

8 Pull back the mat and tidy the ends of the roll. Set aside in a cool place, but not the refrigerator, while you prepare 2 more rolls. Use a knife moistened with vinegared water to cut the rolls in half. Cut each half into 4 slices. When you get more confident you can place the 2 halves alongside each other and cut them together.

Repair tears by re-rolling in an extra nori sheet

Other recipes

Try substituting any of the fillings with these other options: 60g (2oz) skinless fish fillet, such as salmon, tuna, or red snapper, cut into pencil-thick strips (pp.96–97); 60g (2oz) crabmeat or lobster meat; 30g (1oz) spinach or avocado; or 3 seasoned tofu pouches (p.162), cut into 1cm (½in) strips.

SALMON AND GINGER THICK ROLLS

futo maki zushi

Traditionally, cooked vegetables and omelette are used as fillings for thick rolls, but there are no rules against using fresh fish or shellfish. Here is one suggestion that pairs salmon with refreshing ginger and crisp vegetables.

MAKES 24 pieces | **PREPARATION TIME** 40 minutes, plus sushi rice and ingredient preparation

INGREDIENTS

For the vinegared water

2–3 tbsp rice vinegar

250ml (8fl oz) water

For the sushi rolls

3 nori sheets

1 quantity sushi rice (pp.38–41)

1 avocado, peeled, stoned, and cut into thin strips

90g (3oz) pink sushi ginger or red pickled ginger, well drained

30g (1oz) fine green beans, trimmed and blanched

200g (7oz) skinless salmon fillet, cut into pencil-thick strips

6 asparagus, trimmed and lightly blanched

METHOD

1 Combine the ingredients for the vinegared water in a small bowl, then set aside. Place a nori sheet shiny-side down on a rolling mat, dip your hands in the vinegared water, then evenly spread one-third of the rice over the nori, leaving a 4cm (1¾in) margin uncovered at the top edge.

2 Lay one-third of the avocado strips across the centre of the rice, with one-third of the pickled ginger and one-third of the green beans distributed evenly on either side. Arrange one-third of the salmon below the beans and 2 asparagus spears above the avocado.

3 Place your thumbs under the rolling mat and lift near the edge of the mat with your thumbs and index fingers. Hold the fillings in place with your other fingers. (Also see the rolling technique on pp.202–03.)

4 Holding a flap at the top of the mat, bring the near side of the roll over to cover the fillings. Bring the rolling mat down to meet the strip of nori, and gently squeeze along the length of the roll to tuck in the near edge of the nori.

5 Lift the front edge of the mat slightly with one hand and use the other to gently push the roll forward so that the strip of nori not covered by rice seals the roll.

6 Pull back the mat and tidy the ends of the roll. Set aside in a cool place, but not the refrigerator, while you prepare the remaining 2 rolls. Use a knife moistened with vinegared water to cut the rolls in half. Cut each half into 4 slices.

INSIDE-OUT ROLL SUSHI

uramaki

Despite appearances, this type of rolled sushi is easier to prepare than the traditional nori-outside version. This is because the amount of rice used isn't so crucial, and furthermore, inside-out rolls can be prepared in advance as it is less important for the nori to stay crisp. The "California roll" demonstrated here traditionally contains cooked crabmeat and avocado. It was first created by an American-born Japanese sushi chef in the early 1970s for some of his customers who were less keen to eat raw fish and also didn't like the sensation of biting into crisp nori – it has since become a classic.

MAKES 36 pieces | **PREPARATION TIME** 35 minutes, plus sushi rice and ingredient preparation

INGREDIENTS

For the vinegared water

2–3 tbsp rice vinegar

250ml (8fl oz) water

For the sushi rolls

3 sheets nori seaweed

1 quantity sushi rice
(pp.38–41)

120g (4oz) crabmeat (p.106)

1 baby cucumber or
¼ large cucumber, cut
into pencil-thick strips

120g (4oz) mayonnaise

wasabi paste (optional)

1 medium avocado,
peeled, stoned, and sliced
lengthways into thin strips

6 tbsp flying fish roe

METHOD

1 Mix the ingredients for the vinegared water in a small bowl and set aside. Lay a bamboo rolling mat on your work surface and cover it with cling film. Break a nori sheet in half across the grain and place it on the mat.

CONTINUED ▶

2 Dip your hands in the vinegared water, take a good handful of rice about 100g (3½oz) in weight and place it in the middle of the nori. Use your fingers to spread an even layer of rice to the edges of the nori. Pick up the rice-covered nori and quickly turn it over on the mat.

3 Lay the crab and cucumber along the centre of the nori. Add a line of mayonnaise on one side and a thin smear of wasabi on the other, if using. Arrange the avocado on top.

4 Lift up the near edge of the mat, holding the fillings in place with your fingers, if necessary. Start rolling to join the 2 edges of the rice and nori sheet together.

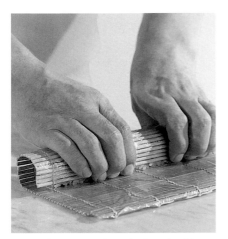

5 Gently squeeze along the length of the roll to mould it together, then lift up the front edge of the mat and push the roll forward to join the 2 edges of nori. Use gentle but firm pressure to shape the log into a round or square shape.

6 Open the mat. Spoon the fish roe onto the sushi roll, and use the back of a spoon to spread the roe over it. Turn the roll over to coat the underneath. The roe does not have to cover the sushi perfectly. Repeat to make 6 sushi rolls.

7 Dip a cloth or tea towel in the vinegared water, use it to moisten a sharp knife, and cut each roll in half. Place the 2 halves next to each other, moisten the knife, and cut twice to give 6 equal-sized pieces per roll.

SPICY CRAYFISH, AVOCADO, AND MANGO INSIDE-OUT ROLLS

This variation on traditional inside-out rolls offers a fresh, tropical twist with slices of fragrant mango, creamy avocado, and a piquant sauce.

MAKES 36 pieces | **PREPARATION TIME** 45 minutes, plus sushi rice and ingredient preparation

INGREDIENTS

For the spicy mayo

6 tbsp mayonnaise

6 tsp chilli sauce

1 tbsp lime juice

3 tsp cayenne pepper

For the vinegared water

2–3 tbsp rice vinegar

250ml (8fl oz) water

For the sushi rolls

3 sheets nori seaweed, each cut in half across the grain

1 quantity sushi rice (pp.38–41)

250g (9oz) cooked crayfish tails or king prawns, well drained

1 mango, peeled, stoned, and cut into thin strips

1 avocado, peeled, stoned, and cut into thin strips

3 tbsp toasted white sesame seeds

3 tbsp toasted black sesame seeds

METHOD

1 Combine the ingredients for the spicy mayo and the vinegared water in separate bowls, then set both aside. Lay a bamboo rolling mat on your work surface, cover it with cling film, and place half a nori sheet on top horizontally.

2 Dip your hands in the vinegared water, then divide the sushi rice into 6 equal portions. Spread one portion of sushi rice in an even layer to the edges of the nori, then pick up the sheet and quickly turn it over on the mat.

3 Lay one-sixth of the crayfish and mango along the centre of the nori. Add a line of the spicy mayo alongside the crayfish. Arrange one-sixth of the avocado on top.

4 Lift up the near edge of the mat, holding the fillings in place with your fingers, if necessary. Start rolling to join the 2 edges of the rice and nori sheet together. (Also see the rolling technique on pp.208–09.)

5 Gently squeeze along the length of the roll to mould it together, then lift up the front edge of the mat and push the roll forward to join the 2 edges of nori. Use gentle but firm pressure to shape the log into a round or square shape.

6 Spread ½ tbsp each of white and black sesame seeds on a large flat surface, and roll the sushi roll to coat it. Repeat to make 6 sushi rolls.

7 Dip a cloth or tea towel in the vinegared water, use it to moisten a sharp knife, and cut each roll in half. Place the 2 halves next to each other, moisten the knife, and cut twice to give 6 equal-sized pieces per roll.

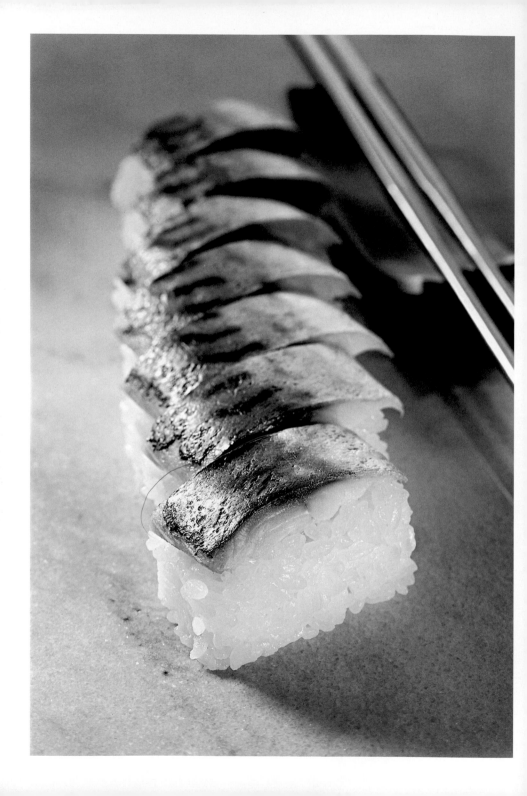

LOG ROLL SUSHI
bō zushi

This simple but delicious rolled sushi uses vinegar-marinated mackerel as
a wrapping material instead of nori. It is an excellent way to enjoy the taste of
marinated mackerel if you don't have a pressed sushi mould to make *battera*
(pp.182–85). Be sure to leave adequate time to prepare the fish (pp.100–101),
and let the roll stand for 20–30 minutes at room temperature before cutting
as this allows time for the flavours to develop.

MAKES 16 pieces | **PREPARATION TIME** 45 minutes, plus sushi rice and ingredient preparation

INGREDIENTS

For the vinegared water

2–3 tbsp rice vinegar

250ml (8fl oz) water

For the sushi rolls

1 quantity sushi rice
(pp.38–41)

2 vinegar-marinated
mackerel fillets (pp.100–101),
about 150g (5oz) each

wasabi paste (optional)

METHOD

1 Mix the ingredients for the vinegared water in a small
bowl and set aside. Lay a rolling mat on your work
surface and cover both sides of it in cling film.

CONTINUED ▶

2 Wet your hands with vinegared water. Place 2 small handfuls of rice in the centre of the rolling mat and shape into a mackerel-length log.

3 Dab the underside of the mackerel with a little wasabi, if using. Place the fillet on top of the mound of rice, skin-side up.

4 Lift the mat over the rice and mackerel so that it is completely covered.

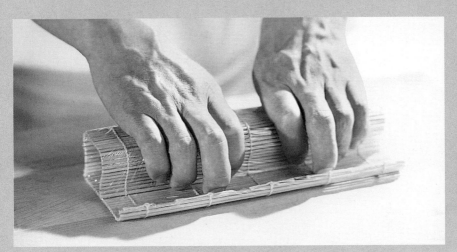

5 Work your hands along the length of the sushi log, squeezing it firmly but gently. If the mackerel is longer than the rice, neaten it by pressing the ends of the fish over so that they stick to the rice. Repeat to make 1 more roll.

6 Set aside to stand for 20–30 minutes at room temperature. Dip a cloth or tea towel in the vinegared water and use to moisten a sharp knife. Cut each log in half, then slice each half into 4 bite-sized pieces.

HAND-ROLLED SUSHI
temaki zushi

This is such a great type of sushi – it's so simple and easy to make, there's no need for a rolling mat, and even children can join in. All you need to do is prepare the rice and fillings and lay them out to let everyone have fun making their own sushi. The only thing to remember is to make sure you have prepared a generous amount because, I guarantee you, they will love it.

MAKES 20 cornets | **PREPARATION TIME** 45 minutes, plus sushi rice and ingredient preparation

INGREDIENTS

10 sheets nori seaweed, halved across the grain

1 quantity sushi rice (pp.38–41)

wasabi paste

400g (14oz) skinless fillet of any fish, preferably of different types, such as tuna and salmon, cut for hand-rolled sushi (pp.96–97)

100g (3½oz) salmon roe or flying fish roe

½ quantity rolled Japanese omelette (pp.44–46)

400g (14oz) vegetables in total, such as steamed carrot, blanched green beans, cucumber, and pickled daikon, cut into pencil-thick strips about 6cm (2½in) long

METHOD

1 Hold a piece of nori in your left hand and put 1 generous tbsp sushi rice in the top left-hand corner.

CONTINUED ▶

2 Spread the rice to the centre of the bottom edge of the nori. Use your finger to flatten the rice slightly, then dab a little wasabi paste on it.

Try vegetables, fish, or both together — anything goes

3 Arrange your choice of fillings on top of the rice so they point diagonally to the top left corner of the nori.

218

4 Fold the bottom left-hand corner of the nori towards the top right-hand corner, wrapping it around the rice and fillings.

Eat right away so the nori stays crisp

5 Continue rolling until the nori forms a cornet shape that holds the rice and fillings.

Other recipes

Try other fish fillings, such as sea bass, red snapper, turbot, brill, lemon sole, vinegar-marinated mackerel (pp.100–101), and smoked salmon. Other good vegetable fillings include avocado, mustard cress, and perilla leaves.

SUSHI BURRITOS

This Mexican–Japanese street food hybrid is an example of innovative, modern sushi. The filling is generous and the rolling technique is similar to that of thick rolls. Here is just one filling suggestion – have fun experimenting with others.

MAKES 4 burrito rolls | **PREPARATION TIME** 40 minutes, plus sushi rice and ingredient preparation

INGREDIENTS

For the sauce

4 tbsp mayonnaise

4 tsp chilli sauce

½ tsp cayenne pepper

2 tbsp toasted white sesame seeds

For the vinegared water

2–3 tbsp rice vinegar

250ml (8fl oz) water

For the burrito rolls

8 sheets nori seaweed

1 quantity sushi rice (pp.38–41)

40g (1¼oz) wild rocket leaves

200g (7oz) skinless salmon fillet, cut into pencil-thick strips (pp.96–97)

1 avocado, peeled, stoned, and sliced lengthways into thin strips

1 cucumber, pulpy centre discarded and cut into pencil-thick strips

METHOD

1 Combine the ingredients for the sauce and the vinegared water in separate bowls, then set both aside. Place 1 nori sheet on a bamboo rolling mat, shiny-side down. Dip your hands in vinegared water, then spread one-quarter of the sushi rice evenly over the nori, leaving a 3–4cm (1–1½in) margin on the edge furthest from you uncovered.

2 Slide the edge of a second nori sheet under the uncovered margin (see below). Spread 1 tbsp of the sauce over the rice, then layer one-quarter of the rocket leaves, salmon, avocado, and cucumber in the centre of the rice.

3 Lift up the near edge of the mat with your thumbs and index fingers. Keeping the filling in place with your other fingers, roll the mat to cover the filling, then lift the front of the mat slightly and push the roll forward to the end.

4 Wrap the burrito in greaseproof paper, twisting each end tightly to keep it in shape. Repeat to make 4 burrito rolls. Cut diagonally in half with a moistened knife to serve.

HOW TO JOIN AN EXTRA NORI SHEET

Add a second nori sheet under the far edge of the first sheet, to create the extra length needed to contain the burrito filling. The moisture from the sushi rice will join the two sheets when rolled.

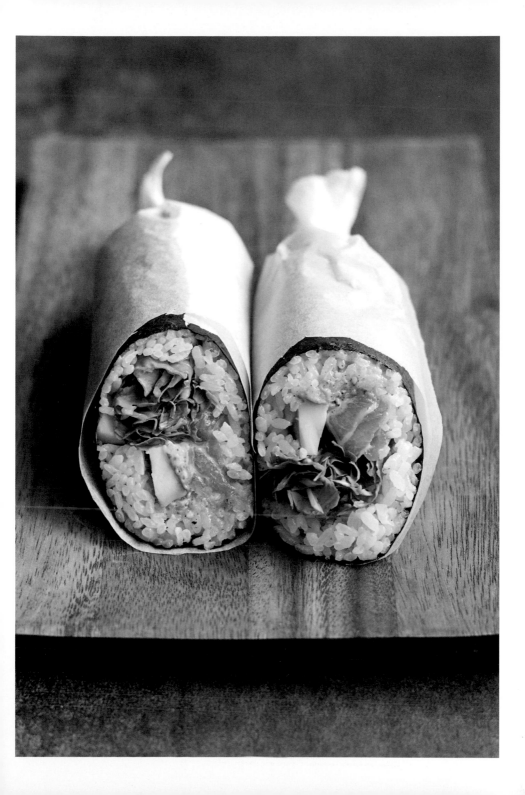

HAND-FORMED SUSHI
nigiri zushi

A relatively **new** addition to the sushi repertoire, *nigiri zushi* is less than 200 years old. It was first invented as a **street food** in the old capital Edo, now Tokyo, and totally **revolutionized** sushi because it took so little time to make. *Nigiri* means "to squeeze" – when a sushi chef makes *nigiri zushi*, he gently squeezes a small quantity of rice into an oval, adds a perfectly judged amount of wasabi paste, then **presses on a topping**, usually of fish. But there is more to it than simply making balls of rice and putting slices of fish on top. The **perfect piece** of *nigiri zushi* should be the **right size** to eat in one mouthful and the rice should gently fall apart on your tongue, not in your fingers or chopsticks. The **gentle tartness** of the sushi rice should complement the topping, not compete with it, and a hint of wasabi should **enhance the flavour**.

Start with Easy Hand-formed Sushi (pp.224–27), and progress to the expert's method (pp.228–31) when you have **perfected the technique**. Also in this section are recipes for two other types of shaped sushi that you can **form by hand** without the use of a mould or a rolling mat: battleship sushi (pp.232-35) and sushi balls (pp.236–39).

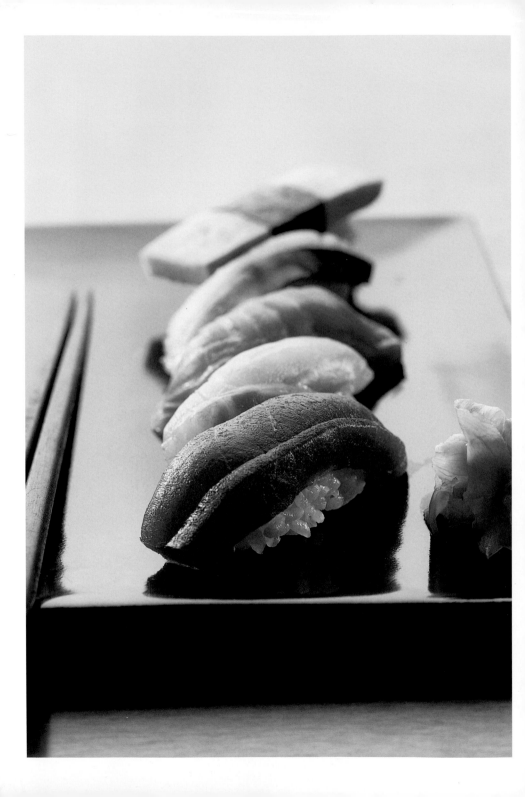

EASY HAND-FORMED SUSHI

nigiri zushi

Out of respect for the art of sushi and its masters, Japanese people rarely make nigiri zushi at home but go to sushi bars to eat it. However, philosophy aside, the assembly itself is fairly easy. Use about 100g (3½oz) of sushi rice per person, which makes roughly five nigiri pieces. Always prepare the toppings before you start and keep a bowl of vinegared water nearby to dip your fingers.

MAKES 24–32 pieces | **PREPARATION TIME** 45 minutes, plus sushi rice and ingredient preparation

INGREDIENTS

For the vinegared water

2–3 tbsp rice vinegar

250ml (8fl oz) water

For the hand-formed sushi

1 quantity sushi rice
(pp.38–41)

400g (14oz) skinless fillet
of any fish, preferably of
different types, such as red
snapper, salmon, and tuna,
cut for hand-formed sushi
(pp.96–97)

wasabi paste

½ quantity rolled Japanese
omelette (pp.44–46), cut into
5mm (¼in) thick slices

5 strips nori seaweed, cut to
1 x 7.5cm (½ x 3in), for tying
the omelette topping

METHOD

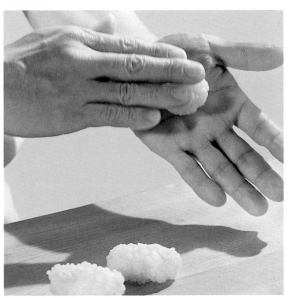

1 Mix the ingredients for the vinegared water in a small bowl. Dip your hands in the mixture (which prevents the rice from sticking to your fingers) and pick up a small ball of rice. Gently roll it in the palm of your hands, shaping it into an oblong. Place it on a clean work surface or chopping board. Prepare several at a time.

CONTINUED ▶

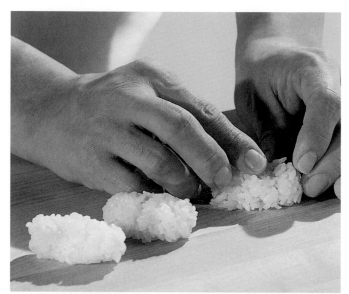

2 Tidy up the shape of the rice balls, if necessary, but don't over-handle the rice.

3 Lay the toppings out next to each oblong of rice. Dab a little wasabi paste on each oblong of rice. Omit wasabi if using omelette as a topping.

4 Lay the topping on each rice oblong, and press gently to keep it in place. Avoid excessive handling of the fish.

5 If using fish as a topping, use your thumb and forefinger to press the ends of the fish to the rice.

6 Gently shape the sides of the rice. If using omelette as a topping, tie the sushi with a strip of nori.

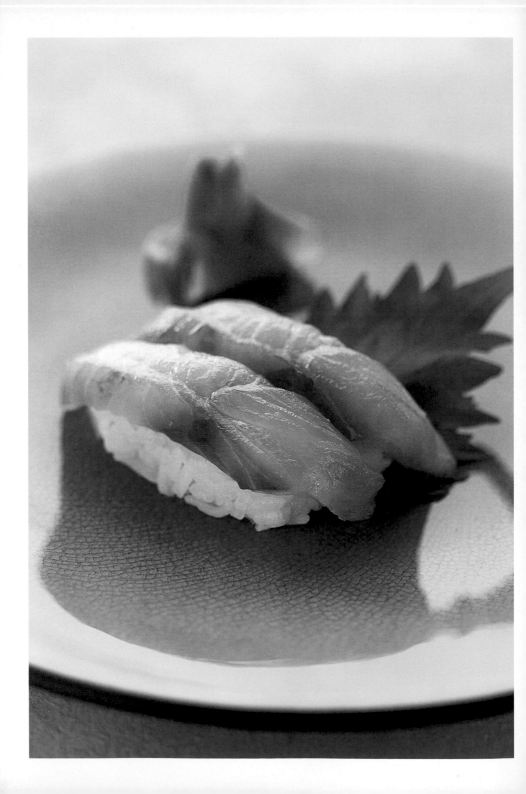

EXPERT HAND-FORMED SUSHI

nigiri zushi

This is the ultimate sushi. A sushi master spends years perfecting his technique and produces each piece of sushi in what appears to be one smooth movement that takes only a matter of seconds. In his expert hands, the pieces tend to be marginally smaller than Easy Hand-formed Sushi (pp.224–27), and use less rice but slightly more fish. As you become more practised at the technique, you will find that you are able to make *nigiri zushi* more quickly.

MAKES 40–50 pieces | **PREPARATION TIME** 30–60 minutes, plus sushi rice and ingredient preparation

INGREDIENTS

For the vinegared water

2–3 tbsp rice vinegar

250ml (8fl oz) water

For the hand-formed sushi

1 quantity sushi rice
(pp.38–41)

500g (1lb) skinless fillet
of any fish, preferably of
different types, such as red
snapper, salmon, tuna, sole,
brill, or sea bass, cut for
hand-formed sushi
(pp.96–97)

wasabi paste

METHOD

1 Mix the ingredients for the vinegared water in a small bowl and wet your hands in it to prevent the rice from sticking to them. Take a small handful of rice in your right hand and gently mould it into a rounded oblong.

CONTINUED ▶

2 Holding the ball of rice loosely in your right fist, pick up the topping with your left hand. Lay the topping across your fingers, and dab a little wasabi paste on it.

3 Hold the rice between your right thumb and index finger, and gently press it onto the topping with your left thumb.

4 Hold the sushi halfway along its sides, between your thumb and index finger. Spin the sushi 180° so the topping is on top.

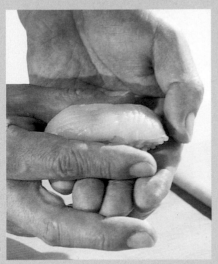

5 Squeeze the sides of the sushi between your right forefinger and thumb to shape it and compact the rice.

6 Cup the sushi in your left hand and use two fingers to press gently on the top to compact it further.

7 Open your left hand and spin the sushi round, keeping the topping on top. Repeat steps 6 and 7 to shape the sushi.

BATTLESHIP SUSHI
gunkan maki

Sushi toppings such as fish roe and oysters simply will not stay on the sushi rice without some form of containment. This type of sushi is called *gunkan maki*, meaning "battleship roll", because the strip of nori seaweed that keeps the topping in place gives it a battleship shape. The nori absorbs the moisture from the rice and the topping and becomes soggy if left too long, so make this type of sushi last if you are making a selection.

MAKES 18 pieces | **PREPARATION TIME** 30 minutes, plus sushi rice and ingredient preparation

INGREDIENTS

For the vinegared water

2–3 tbsp rice vinegar

250ml (8fl oz) water

For the sushi

3 sheets nori seaweed

½ quantity sushi rice
(pp.38–41)

wasabi paste

120g (4oz) flying fish roe,
(can be dyed red, green,
or natural coloured)

6 oysters

60g (2oz) salmon roe

METHOD

1 Mix the ingredients for the vinegared water in a small bowl and set aside. Put the 3 sheets of nori on top of each other and cut them into 6 equal-sized strips about 2.5cm (1in) wide and 15cm (6in) long.

CONTINUED ▶

2 Wet your hands in the vinegared water. Shape about 1 tbsp sushi rice into an oblong-shaped ball. Wipe one of your hands dry and pick up a strip of nori. Wrap it around the rice ball with the smooth side of the nori facing outwards.

3 Crush a grain of cooked rice at the end of the strip of nori so that it sticks the nori down where it overlaps to form a ring around the rice.

Wrap the nori with a dry hand to keep it crisp

234

4 Dab a little wasabi paste on the rice and flatten the rice slightly.

5 Spoon the topping onto the rice, keeping it inside the ring of nori.

SUSHI BALLS

temari zushi

These delectable sushi balls are the nearest sushi style to nigiri zushi but are far easier to make, requiring neither specialist equipment nor years of training. All you need is cling film or a handkerchief to shape the balls.

MAKES 20–30 pieces | **PREPARATION TIME** 25 minutes, plus sushi rice and ingredient preparation

INGREDIENTS

30g (1oz) smoked salmon, cut into 10 postage stamp-size pieces

½ quantity sushi rice (pp.38–41)

10 cooked prawns

30g (1oz) flying fish roe or caviar

wasabi paste

METHOD

1 Lay a piece of cling film (or a clean, damp handkerchief; see Method, p.238) about 10cm (4in) square on a clean work surface and place a piece of smoked salmon at the centre of it. Mould 1 heaped tsp of sushi rice into a loose ball and place on top of the smoked salmon.

2 Pick up all four corners of the cling film and gather them in the middle. Twist the cling film to compact the rice and form a small ball. Repeat the process to make 10 smoked salmon balls. Make 10 prawn balls in the same way, but put ½ tsp flying fish roe or caviar in the cresent of each prawn.

3 Keep each piece of sushi wrapped in the cling film until just before serving. Put a dab of wasabi on each of the smoked salmon balls just before serving.

HOW TO SHAPE THE BALLS

The name temari means handball

Form the rice into a loose ball, but don't overhandle it.

Adjust the shape of the ball with your fingers, if necessary.

MIX-AND-MATCH SUSHI BALLS
temari zushi

These cute, pretty sushi balls are a favourite for *hinamatsuri*, or Girls' Day, celebrations in Japan. Make them as a starter dish for your own festivities with a variety of colourful toppings, and serve them mix-and-match style.

MAKES 32 pieces | **PREPARATION TIME** 30 minutes, plus sushi rice and ingredient preparation

INGREDIENTS

100g (3½oz) skinless fillet of salmon

100g (3½oz) skinless fillet of tuna

100g (3½oz) skinless fillet of white fish, such as sea bass, sea bream, or lemon sole

8 cooked king or tiger prawns

wasabi paste

1 quantity sushi rice (pp.38–41)

8 perilla leaves or coriander leaves

Other recipes
You can make sushi balls with many other toppings, including: thin omelette (p.43), ham, cucumber, rare roast beef (all these should be sliced thinly and cut to postage stamp-size pieces), or use any variety of caviar.

METHOD

1 Start by cutting the fish as for hand-formed sushi, into slices about 5mm (¼in) thick (pp.96–97). Cut 8 slices of each fish. (The quantity of fish suggested is more than you need because it is easier to work with a larger amount; you could use any extra slices in the Wafer-thin Sashimi recipe on page 248.)

2 Shell, clean, and butterfly the cooked prawns (pp.118–19). Remove the tail shells.

3 Place a clean, damp handkerchief (or a piece of cling film; see Method, p.236) on the palm of your hand, and put a piece of fish on top. Smear a pinhead of wasabi paste on the fish. Using a wet dessertspoon, take a large spoonful of the sushi rice (about 20g /³⁄₄oz) and put it on top of the fish.

4 Pick up all four corners of the handkerchief and gather them in the middle over the rice. Twist tightly to compact the rice into a small ball, roughly the size of a ping-pong ball. Unwrap the sushi ball and place it on a plate while you repeat the process to make 8 sushi balls for each variety of fish and the prawns.

5 For the white fish, make 8 sushi balls in the same way, but place a perilla leaf on top of the fish before adding the rice. When you have formed the sushi ball, the green colour of the leaf will show through the white fish.

SASHIMI
an introduction

The Japanese believe that in most cases the less a food is cooked the better, and the **best way** to cook a fish is **not to cook** it at all. To some, sashimi looks like sushi without the rice, but there is more to it than **sliced raw fish**. Sashimi is one of the **oldest** Japanese cuisines and has a history all of its own.

In 123CE, the reigning Emperor was served raw bonito and clams with vinegar by his head chef – this was sashimi in its earliest form. By the middle of the 15th century, *namasu*, as it was then known, was eaten with **seasoned vinegar**, not with soy sauce as it is today. By the mid-17th century, sea bass, red snapper, bonito, shark, eel, perch, carp, shellfish, pheasant, and duck were all used for sashimi. Many of these were eaten **raw** but some were **blanched** or **lightly cooked**. At around the same time, **soy sauce** became widely available, and sashimi, in the form that we know today, became popular.

Today, sashimi is regarded as the **perfect start** to a Japanese meal. It is served with soy sauce, wasabi, shredded daikon, and sometimes fresh seaweed and perilla leaves – accompaniments chosen not just for their colours and flavours but for their **ability to aid digestion**.

CLASSIC SASHIMI PLATE

Generally, any fish that is suitable for sushi can also be used for sashimi. The most crucial factor is freshness, even more so than for sushi, as with sashimi there are no other ingredients to disguise the fish's flavour. For an attractive arrangement, choose fish with both red and white meat and decorate the plate with a few carefully chosen garnishes. You should allow about 120g (4oz) fish per person.

SERVES 4 | **PREPARATION TIME** 1 hour, plus freezing time

INGREDIENTS

8 *ama ebi* (raw prawns in a sugar-vinegar glaze, available from Japanese fishmongers), or cooked coldwater prawns, shelled but with tails on

120g (4oz) sole or sea bass fillet, about 7.5cm (3in) wide

two 7.5cm (3in) pieces of cucumber, one of them cut into 4 pine branch garnishes (p.50)

7.5cm (3in) piece of fresh daikon, peeled

120g (4oz) white fish fillet, such as red snapper, sea bass, or sea bream

250g (9oz) fish fillets with red meat, such as tuna, mackerel, salmon, or bonito

4 perilla leaves

4 sea urchins (optional)

4 wasabi leaves (p.51)

12 thin slices of lemon or lime

2 tsp flying fish roe

METHOD

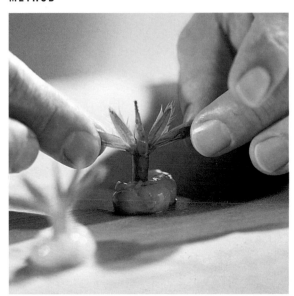

1 First, shape the prawns into fantails. Lay a prawn on its side on a chopping board. Hold it by its tail and twist so that the body coils around the tail. Separate the individual shell pieces in the tail to make a decorative fan. Repeat with the remaining prawns.

CONTINUED ▶

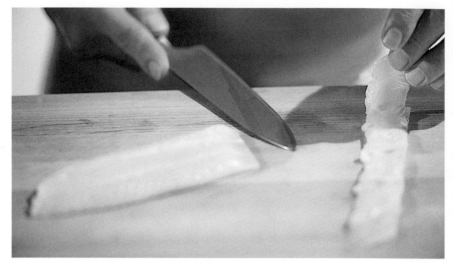

2 Form the sole or sea bass fillet into "roses", but first semi-freeze the fish for 15–30 minutes to make it firmer and easier to slice. Slice the fillet at a 45° angle and cut 12–16 thin slices as for hand-formed sushi (see p.96, Step 1). Lay 3–4 slices lengthways in a line, with each slice overlapping by about 2.5cm (1in).

3 Roll up the line of fish slices. Use chopsticks, if necessary, to pick up the ends of each slice and to roll it.

4 Set the rose on its base, and use chopsticks or your fingers to gently shape the "petals". Repeat to make 4 roses.

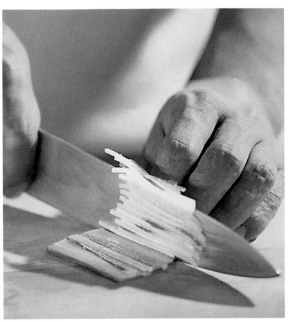

5 Shred the pieces of cucumber and daikon into very fine strands (see p.49). Soak the shredded vegetables in a bowl of cold water for 10 minutes before draining. Meanwhile, prepare the remaining fish fillets.

A sharp knife will cut the fish cleanly

6 To prepare the white fish and the fish with red meat, slice the fillets straight down at a 90° angle into 8mm–1cm (⅓–½in) thick pieces. Lastly, assemble the sashimi on 4 individual plates. Place 3–4 little heaps of cucumber and daikon on each plate and use them as "beds" to display 1 perilla leaf, 1 cucumber pine branch, and the red and white fish slices on each plate. Arrange 1 sea urchin, 1 white fish rose, 2 prawn fantails, 1 wasabi leaf, and 3 citrus slices artistically on each plate. Place ½ tsp flying fish roe on top of each white fish rose, and serve.

CUBED TUNA SASHIMI WITH WASABI-AVOCADO DRESSING
Maguro no kaku-zukuri

Kaku-zukuri, or cube cut, is arguably the easiest style of sashimi cut, especially in the West where tuna is often sold in steak form. This style of sashimi is suitable for soft-fleshed, oily fish such as tuna, salmon, yellowtail, or bonito.

SERVES 4　|　**PREPARATION TIME** 15 minutes

INGREDIENTS

For the wasabi-avocado dressing

1 very ripe avocado, peeled and stoned

4 tbsp rice vinegar

1 tbsp wasabi paste

1 tbsp light soy sauce

For the sashimi

2 tuna steaks, each about 2cm (¾in) thick and weighing about 400g (14oz)

1 tsp toasted white sesame seeds

1 tsp toasted black sesame seeds

1 spring onion, finely sliced

METHOD

1 To make the wasabi-avocado dressing, chop the avocado into small chunks and press through a sieve to purée. In a large non-reactive bowl, combine the avocado purée with the vinegar, wasabi, and soy sauce, and mix well.

2 Cut the tuna steaks into 2cm (¾in) wide strips along the sinews, then rotate the strips 90° and cut straight down at 2cm (¾in) intervals to form cubes.

3 Divide the tuna cubes among 4 serving plates. Drizzle the wasabi-avocado dressing over the tuna (you can use a piping bag to achieve a uniform drizzle, if you wish), sprinkle with the white and black toasted sesame seeds, and garnish with the spring onion. Serve immediately.

WAFER-THIN SASHIMI OF SEA BASS WITH SPICY SOY DRESSING
Hirame no usu-zukuri

Usu-zukuri, or wafer-thin cut, is a sashimi style suitable for firm-fleshed white fish, such as sea bass or sea bream, or for smaller flatfish such as plaice and turbot. In Japan, it is a traditional, seasonal treat to eat blowfish made in this way. Consider this Japan's answer to Italian carpaccio or Peruvian ceviche.

SERVES 4　|　**PREPARATION TIME** 15 minutes, plus freezing time

INGREDIENTS

For the sashimi

400g (14oz) sea bass fillets, skin and bones removed

4 spring onions, finely sliced lengthways, to garnish

For the spicy soy dressing

1 garlic clove, grated

½–1 red chilli, deseeded and very finely chopped

grated zest and juice of 1 unwaxed lemon

4 tbsp soy sauce

METHOD

1 Place the fish fillets (each wrapped in cling film) in the freezer for 10–15 minutes, or until they are semi-frozen and firm enough to be sliced easily, but not frozen solid; keep checking. Chill 4 serving plates in the refrigerator.

2 Meanwhile, mix all the dressing ingredients in a small bowl and set aside. Take out the chilling plates and the fish. Unwrap the fish and place it on a chopping board.

3 With the skinned-side up, cut the fish into wafer-thin slices about 3mm (⅛in) thick (see below). Carefully arrange the slices in an overlapping pattern on each serving plate. Drizzle the soy dressing over, garnish with the spring onions, and serve immediately.

HOW TO CUT WAFER-THIN SLICES

Place the fillet at an angle, with the thin end closest to you. Starting at the thin end, hold the knife almost horizontal and draw the blade in a smooth, diagonal movement to produce a thin slice. Support the top of the slice with your fingertips as you cut.

GLOSSARY

Abura age Puffy, brown deep-fried tofu (p.162)

Agari Green tea served in sushi bars

Aji Spanish or horse wckerel (p.62)

Akami Lean tuna, cut from the back of the fish (p.68)

Ama ebi Sweet shrimp, usually served raw (p.116)

Asari Common clam (p.132)

Battera Marinated mackerel pressed sushi (p.70, 182)

Bīru Beer (p.14)

Bō zushi Log roll sushi (p.212)

Chakin zushi "Stuffed purse" sushi (p.168)

Chirashi zushi Scattered sushi (p.136)

Chū toro Medium fatty tuna, from the upper belly (p.68)

Daikon Long white radish (p.34) also known as mouli

Dashi Basic fish stock (p.47)

Dashi maki tamago Rolled, sweet omelette (p.44)

Deba bōchō Type of knife – cleaver (p.21)

Edomae chirashi zushi Tokyo-style scattered sushi (p.138)

Fukin Cloth used in the kitchen (p.22)

Fukusa zushi Sushi wrapped in a pancake omelette (p.170)

Futo maki Thick roll sushi also known as date maki (p.200)

Gari Pickled ginger (p.29)

Gomoku zushi Scattered sushi – "five item sushi" (p.144)

Gunkan maki Nigiri sushi wrapped with nori to hold loose toppings (p.232)

Hamachi Yellowtail tuna (p.133)

Hangiri Wooden rice tub (p.22)

Hashi Chopsticks

Hikari mono Term for shiny, oily fish (p.62, 64)

Hirame Term for flatfish with eyes on the left side of the head (p.84, 86)

Hōchō General term for knives (p.21)

Hoso maki Thin roll sushi (p.196)

Hotate gai Scallops (p.126, 129)

Ika Squid (pp.120–23)

Ikura Salmon roe (p.130)

Inari zushi Deep-fried tofu (*abura age*) stuffed with sushi rice (p.160, 162)

Iri goma Toasted sesame seeds (p.32), can be white or black

Ise ebi Lobster (p.112–15)

Itamae Professional chef

Iwashi Sardine (p.64)

Kaki Oysters (p.126, 128)

Kampyō Strips of dried gourd (p.24, 31)

Kani Crab (p.106–11, 133)

Karei Term for flatfish with eyes on the right side of the head (p.88, 90)

Katsuo Bonito (p.66)

Katsuo bushi Dried bonito flakes (p.33, 47)

Kazunoko Herring roes (p.64, 131)

Kome Japanese-style rice (p.26)

Konbu Kelp, usually dried (p.33)

Maguro Tuna (p.68)

Maki zushi Rolled sushi, called *nori maki* if made with nori seaweed (p.194)

Makisu Mat made of bamboo strips for making roll sushi (p.20, 194)

Matō dai John Dory (p.74)

Matsukawa "Pine bark method" of fish skin zukuri (p.102)

Mirin Sweet rice wine for cooking (p.30)

Miso shiru Soup made with soy bean paste (p.54)

Nigiri zushi Hand-formed sushi rice topped with fish, vegetables, or omelette (p.228)

Nishin Herring (p.64)

Nori Dark seaweed pressed into thin sheets (p.27)

Ō toro Fattiest cut of tuna (p.68)

Ohyō garei Halibut (p.90)

Omakase Chef's choice

Oshibako Pressed sushi mould (p.23, 180)

Oshibori Moistened heated towel

Oshi zushi Pressed sushi (p.180)

Renkon Lotus roots (p.35)

Saba Mackerel (p.70)

Sai bashi Cooking chopsticks

Sake Rice wine (p. 14, 30) – the same word is used for salmon (p.72)

Sanmai oroshi Three-piece filleting technique for round fish (p.80)

Sashimi Sliced or prepared raw fish (p.240)

Shako Mantis shrimp (p.133)

Shamoji Flat rice-serving spoon (p.22)

Shari Term for sushi rice

Shiitake Type of Japanese mushroom (p.32)

Shime saba Vinegar-marinated mackerel (p.100)

Shiso Japanese mint, perilla (p.35)

Shita birame Dover sole (p.133)

Shōyu Japanese soy sauce (p.12, 29)

Su Rice vinegar (p.30)

Sui mono Clear soup (p.52)

Sushi meshi Prepared rice for sushi (p.38)

Suzuki Sea bass (p.76)

Tai (also **Ma dai)** Japanese red snapper (p.78, 102)

Tako Octopus (p.120)

Tamago soboro Scrambled eggs (p.42)

Tamari Wheat-free soy sauce (p.29)

Tataki Cooking method – rapid searing then cooling of the meat (p.142, 155)

Temaki-zushi Hand rolled sushi (p.216)

Temari zushi Sushi balls (p.236–39)

Teriyaki sauce Thicker, sweetened soy sauce (p.177)

Tobiko Flying fish roe (p.131)

Tofu Soybean curd (p.54)

Toro Fatty tuna – *see* chu toro, oho toro

Tsuma / kazari Garnishes / decorations (pp.48–51)

Uni Sea urchin (p.130)

Uramaki Inside-out roll sushi (p.206)

Usuba bōchō Vegetable knife (p.21)

Usuyaki tamago Thin, pancake omelette (p.43)

Wakiita "Side chopping board" or assistant sushi chef

Wasabi Green, hot Japanese type of horseradish (p.28)

Yanagi bōchō Fish knife (p.21)

Zaru Bamboo strainer or basket

Zāsai Chinese pickled vegetable (p.190)

INDEX

Page numbers in **bold** refer to main entries; entries in *italics* indicate recipes.

Project Editor Shashwati Tia Sarkar
Project Art Editor Vicky Read
Senior Jackets Creative Nicola Powling
Senior Producer, Pre-Production Tony Phipps
Pre-Production Assitant Marina Hartung
Senior Producer Ché Creasey
Managing Editor Dawn Henderson
Managing Art Editor Marianne Markham
Art Director Maxine Pedliham
Publishing Director Mary-Clare Jerram

DK INDIA
Project Editor Janashree Singha
Senior Art Editor Ira Sharma
Managing Editor Soma B. Chowdhury
Managing Art Editor Arunesh Talapatra
Pre-Production Manager Sunil Sharma
DTP Designer Satish Chandra Gaur

First Edition
Project Editor Hugh Thompson
Project Art Editor Sara Robin
Book Editor Nasim Mawji
Designer Colin Goody
Managing Editor Gillian Roberts
Category Publisher Mary-Clare Jerram
Art Director Tracy Killick
DTP Designers Sonia Charbonnier, Louise Waller
Production Controller Louise Daly

This edition published in Great Britain in 2017 by
Dorling Kindersley Limited, 80 Strand, London WC2R 0RL

First edition published in Great Britain in 2002

Copyright © 2002, 2011, 2017 Dorling Kindersley Limited
Text Copyright © 2002, 2011, 2017 Kimiko Barber
A Penguin Random House company
1 3 6 8 10 9 7 5 2
001–262234–July/2017

All rights reserved. No part of this publication may be reproduced,
stored in a retrieval system, or transmitted in any form or by any means
electronic, mechanical, photocopying, recording, or otherwise, without
the prior written permission of the copyright owner.

A CIP catalogue record for this book
is available from The British Library

ISBN 978-0-2413-0110-4

Printed and bound in China
All images © Dorling Kindersley Limited
For further information see: www.dkimages.com

A WORLD OF IDEAS:
SEE ALL THERE IS TO KNOW

www.dk.com

THE AUTHORS

Kimiko Barber

Kimiko left her native Japan to go to an English boarding school in 1972, and quickly realized that she would have to recall her grandmothers' cooking skills if she was to survive. After over ten years working in finance in Tokyo and London, a chance visit to Books for Cooks, a mecca for foodies, inspired her to change her career and focus on cooking and entertaining. Kimiko now writes books and articles about Japanese cuisine and inspires others with her demonstrations of Japanese cooking at various cookery schools around the UK.

Hiroki Takemura

Hiroki completed a sushi chef apprenticeship in Osaka, Japan. To broaden his experience, he then moved to Europe and arrived in a cold and rainy London in February 1982 with just a small suitcase and his sushi knives. For the next ten years he worked in the city's noted Japanese restaurants. In 1996, Nobu Matsuhisa asked Takemura to head up Nobu London's opening team. Takemura accepted, and then worked briefly in Nobu's New York restaurant, to attune himself with the cooking (Takemura still refers to Nobu Matsuhisa as "oyaji" – "honourable father"). Takemura is now Executive Chef at the Sunset Grill & Bar in Istanbul, Turkey.

ACKNOWLEDGMENTS

For the 2002 Edition

Kimiko Barber would like to thank Rosie and Eric of Books for Cooks who supported me throughout and without whose help this book would not have started. A big thank you to Ian O'Leary and his French assistant, Ludo, for taking beautiful photographs and providing good music during the long photo shoot. I also would like to thank all the members of the team of Dorling Kindersley but especially Mary-Clare Jerram, Tracy Killick, Sara Robin, and Hugh Thompson for their very professional but human support. A huge gratitude goes to Nasim Mawji for her transatlantic editing. My special thank you to Jasper Morris of

Morris & Verdin (Wine Merchants) for sharing his wine expertise. Thank you to Kalpana Brijnath, Eve Pleming and Simon May for lending me 'hands' for the party photo shoot. But my final and biggest thank you goes to my long-suffering English husband, Stephen, for his unlimited support and Maxi, Frederick and Dominic, my three sons for being tireless guinea pigs.

DK would like to thank Jenny Jones for her editorial work at the beginning, Rosie Hopper for her inspirational work as a stylist, and Valerie Chandler for the index. The following suppliers kindly provided props: Ceramica Blue (www.ceramicablue.co.uk); New Wave Tableware supplied by Villeroy and Boch (www.villeroy-boch.co.uk); The Conran Shop Ltd (www.conran.com); Handmade boat dishes by Sarah Vernon (www.sarahvernonceramics.com). Many thanks also to Jasper Morris of Fields, Morris & Verdin (www.fmv.co.uk) for his expertise and donating all the wines for the photo shoot.

For the 2017 Edition

DK would like to thank Will Heap for new recipe photography, Seiko Hatfield for food styling, Rob Merrett for prop styling, Jan Fullwood for recipe testing, Corinne Masciocchi and Janashree Singha for proofreading, and Marie Lorimer for the index.

Picture credits: 6bl, 8bl Dorling Kindersley: Peter Wilson, 66-67 123RF.com: PaylessImages, 248b Dorling Kindersley: Quentin Bacon / Masaharu Morimoto. All other images © Dorling Kindersley
For further information see: www.dkimages.com

DISCLAIMER:
Every effort has been made to ensure the information in this book is accurate. However, the publisher is not responsible for your specific health or allergy needs that may require medical supervision, nor for your purchase, handling, or consumption of seafood, whether raw or cooked, nor for any adverse reactions to the recipes contained in this book. Neither the authors nor the publisher will be liable for any loss or damage allegedly arising from any information or suggestion in this book. The authors and publisher advocate sustainable food choices, and every effort has been made to include only sustainable foods in this book. Food sustainability is, however, a shifting landscape, and so we encourage readers to keep up to date with advice on this subject, so that they are equipped to make their own ethical choices.